ENVISION

with

GOD

BELIEVE AND SEE

Francis S. Oda

ISBN 978-1-0980-1575-6 (paperback)
ISBN 978-1-0980-1567-1 (digital)

Christian Faith Publishing
832 Park Avenue
Meadville, PA 16335
www.christianfaithpublishing.com

Printed in the United States of America

ENVISION WITH GOD

BY FRANCIS ODA

"*Believing is seeing.*" This simple twist on the well-known phrase, seeing is believing, has turned people's lives around the world upside down. No longer dependent on what the physical eye sees, Francis Oda encourages all of us to believe first and then see. This shift in perspective requires an intentional, daily time of envisioning with God, who wants to do immeasurably more than we ask or imagine.

Not only does Francis tell us how to envision with God, but he also gives us real-life examples of ordinary people doing extraordinary things. If you have a deep desire for the "immeasurably more," then *Envision with God* is a book that will turn every day of your life into an adventure of faith. As you envision with God, be expectant for the extraordinary. I know I am.

Graham Power
Chairman, Power Group
Founder, Global Day of Prayer and Unashamedly Ethical

****

In his book *Envision with God*, Francis Oda reignites vision, faith and hope, and demonstrates God's resource and provision to see His will done in the life of every believer here on earth!

Francis illustrates masterfully that those of us who consider ourselves "ordinary" have access to the envisioning power of the Holy Spirit to see extraordinary miracles in our homes, our workplaces, churches, streets, cities, regions and nations. In these pages you'll find examples and testimonies of others around the world who have envisioned the "impossible" and seen it happen!

Once you read this book and apply the principles and lifestyle, your life will not be the same!

Derk Maat
Chair, Transform Our World Canada
CEO, SciCorp International

****

As a pastor, one of the questions people most frequently ask me is, "How can I know God's will for my life?" They usually expect some short quick-fix answer as they pass me on their way out of church after a Sunday morning service. Of course, there is nothing I can say in a few words to help them...until now. "Read this book!" will be my reply.

Having heard Francis teach on "Envisioning with God" for several years, I have found his guidance to be some of the best advice for anyone wanting to know how to follow God's leading for their life. As you begin to apply the principles laid out by Francis in *Envision with God*, you will embark on a journey that will help you to develop a lifestyle where extraordinary miracles become the norm rather than the exception.

Brian J. Burton
Senior Pastor, Phuket Christian Centre

****

I don't know of any other book that is so easy and delightful to read, as well as profound and life-changing, as this one. Where else are you going to find terms and concepts like *the practice of dreaming desires, emptying your mind, monkey mind, envision a shelf, spiritual muscles, shot gun prayers and neuroplasticity,* among others, and all within a perfect balance of the Word of God focusing on envisioning with him. *Envision with God* is not only an especially useful and powerful tool, but also a way of life! Once you understand and practice it, your life will never be the same.

I have known Francis for more than 20 years and have benefited personally and collectively, not only from his love and friendship, but from his wholehearted commitment to follow God, his impeccable integrity, his wise counsel, his strong leadership, his noticeable humility and, of course, his wonderful marriage with Caroline. When I listened to this amazing teaching about envisioning with God for the first time, I immediately started applying it in my own life and ministry, and since then it has been a major component in everything I do. My prayer is that as you go through the book, your life will be as touched, inspired, and impacted as mine. Enjoy and prepare for a wonderful and amazing journey as you *Envision with God!*

Poncho Murguia
Director, Transform Our World Mexico

****

Francis Oda has been a close friend for more than three decades. My admiration has grown as I observed him as a follower of Jesus with a quiet, strong integrity. I have also witnessed his expertise as a great architect, and his entrepreneurial skill, embedded with his spiritual gifts, calling and love for God and mankind, is a showcase of service in his office, family and church.

Here's why you will be inspired by this book:

God is creative! We learn that in the first chapter of the Bible, and we are made in His image, allowed to create with Him. In *Envision with God*, Francis shows how you too can create with God in your sphere of influence. One of the most creative men I've known, he has designed some of the most outstanding buildings of the Honolulu skyline while glorifying our Father with his artistry.

Francis writes as a leader among leaders in his field. Read his book and you'll learn how success came over a lifetime of faithfulness to Jesus, practicing His presence daily (both publicly and privately), listening constantly, and obeying His voice!

Loren Cunningham
Founder, Youth with a Mission

FOREWORD

BY DR. ED SILVOSO

W hen it comes to envisioning with God for day-to-day endeavors, Francis Oda speaks with the authority that comes from knowing how to seek and experience God's guidance consistently in his private and professional life—a discipline that turned a young architect in the 1970s into one of the most respected architects today. His world-renowned cultural and environmentally sensitive style of architecture has embellished skylines and laid the foundation for entire communities across the Pacific Rim, from Hawaii to Indonesia and beyond. But it all began with a first step. In *Envision with God,* Francis recounts details of those early days to show how to appropriate the same truths so that you, too, can reach the fullness of God's destiny for you.

As followers of Jesus Christ, we believe that God cares for us because we know that he gave his only begotten son to die on the Cross for our sins. We joyfully relive the moment when he came into our hearts and dissipated our darkness with his divine light. As we grow in the faith, we learn that he also has a hope and a future for us, that his plans for us are for good and not for evil. But often, when facing challenges for which we lack an immediate answer, the question arises, *how can we know what the will of God is for those challenges, not so much when we are in church, but in the workplace? How can we receive his guidance for everyday matters?*

This book answers those questions! The Bible states in unequivocal terms that God's Word is a lamp unto our feet and a light unto our path (Psalm 119:105). This verse speaks of how we can journey to our divine destiny when we find ourselves lacking direction for the next step. Visualize for a moment those exotic Asian shoes pictured in the movies that have an orifice on the tip in which to fit a candle. Imagine yourself wearing a pair of them. With each step you take, the light from the candle reveals where to plant your foot. As you do this one step at a time, you find yourself making steady progress toward the intended destination.

In *Envision with God*, Francis shows in imaginative and practical ways how to take those steps every day until it becomes a lifestyle. Yes! A lifestyle of envisioning with none other than God, hearing from him, being the recipient of his wisdom so that you can successfully and consistently meet daily challenges with divine answers.

We can all recall at least one instance when God intervened in our life in a dramatic way by providing supernatural guidance to solve problems that humanly speaking had no solution. Francis shows that those should not be isolated or rare experiences. On the contrary, they should be part of our daily walk with God. By extracting the practice of envisioning from the realm of the mystical and ethereal, he reveals that it is not a spiritual gift entrusted to some, but rather a discipline that produces results for every believer that engages in it.

This book has the potential to change your life forever. *I wholeheartedly invite you to turn the page and let the journey to your future begin!*

PREFACE

Are you walking into your future backward? If, like many people, you view your future in terms of past experiences, relationships, education, and knowledge, you are probably walking backward! As a result, you may be stumbling and groping your way or tripping blindly over unseen ledges because you're looking in the wrong direction!

God's intention is to turn you around to look squarely into your future through God's eyes. This is envisioning with God!

After all, don't all God's promises lie in the future? Imagine knowing what God speaks of in scripture. "'For I know the plans I have for you,' declares the Lord, 'plans to prosper you and not to harm you, plans to give you hope and a future'" (Jeremiah 29:11, NIV). This book is dedicated to help you envision God's plans to give you a hope and a future!

Jesus said of the Holy Spirit that "He will tell you what is yet to come" (John 16:13, NIV). It is through the Holy Spirit that we can envision with God.

Are you often *deaf* to your future, in addition to being blind? By this I mean that you may not have any confidence as to whether it's God's voice you hear or the flesh, Satan or the pizza eaten last night.

Envisioning with God solves this problem that plagues many sincere believers. It will cause you to recognize the voice of God consistently! If you want to walk into your future *seeing* and *hearing*, I ask you to believe that you will! As you read on, you will see that believing is seeing and not the other way around. *You must believe to see!*

The practice of envisioning with God is not something to be done occasionally, just when a major issue erupts, but should lead to creating a lifestyle of alignment with God's prophetic purpose for you. It is a daily practice that will not only change your life but guide the shaping of your life into what God envisions for you! You will not just be the receiver of God's visions, but be a faithful manifestation of God's vision!

CHAPTER 1

God's Vision

Where there is no vision, the people perish.
— Proverbs 29:18 (KJV)

All In

Crawling in traffic along the freeway to downtown Honolulu, I grappled with a dilemma. About three months earlier, my wife Caroline and I had become Christians. We had spent our first seven years of marriage in the Bay Area with Caroline going to graduate school, and then both of us working.

We lived in San Francisco during the summer of love, the anti-Vietnam War demonstrations, and in Berkeley during the riots! *We loved it!*

Returning to Hawaii to have a family, we were seekers but not finders. We were raised in a traditional Christian denomination but had renounced it when it was discovered ministers of our small San Francisco church were having extramarital relationships with members. After all, this was San Francisco during the heyday of hippiedom, but this was too much for us. We dismissed the Christians as hypocrites and then sought enlightenment in Zen meditation, encounter, human potential movements, but nothing stuck.

In our early thirties, we happened into a movement called EST. We thought this was it! Caroline's good friend Virgie, and her husband Mark, were also in the movement. This led to our having dinner with Virgie's brother Roy and his wife Joan, who had just returned from Cincinnati. We were going to talk them into joining EST.

As the evening progressed, a strange thing happened. The very attributes we were trying to gain from EST, we saw in Roy and Joan. We asked Roy what had changed them in Cincinnati. He told us about their son, Robert, who was born with the umbilical cord wrapped around his neck. As a result, Robert was severely challenged physically, mentally, and developmentally.

For three years, our friends went to every medical center that might be able to help Robert. Roy was a chemical engineer with a good job and the means to afford the best care for Robert, but no one could help him. Then one day, a business friend told him to go to a certain church in Cincinnati where they prayed for healing. Roy asked him how he knew since he was Jewish. The friend said that he didn't go to the church but donated to it because it helped his business! This struck Roy, who was from a Buddhist family, as being very strange, but as a father he was willing to do anything to help Robert. He and Joan went to the service of this large church and went forward with Robert for prayer. By their account, *Robert immediately began to heal!*

They went home rejoicing for the healing but totally bewildered. With the logic of an engineer, Roy said that there were two options. One was that there was no relationship between the prayer and Robert's healing; it was just a coincidence. The other was that there was a connection that they didn't understand and should investigate.

They felt that the second option was the only intellectually honest choice, so they began to attend services. Not only did they give their lives to Jesus, but within a few years Roy became a leader in the church. Then God told them to return to Hawaii. Roy didn't want to return because he knew his father would disown him for becoming a Christian, *which His father did!* (Ultimately, Roy's whole family, including his mother and father, came to the Lord.)

After arguing with God for months, Roy and Joan finally relented and returned. It was within a couple of weeks of their return that we had this fateful dinner with them.

Believe and See

After listening to Roy's story, Caroline asked if they had found a church in Honolulu. They said that they had. Caroline asked to go to a church service with them! I was totally floored! Why go to church with a bunch of hypocrites? Hadn't we burned this bridge in San Francisco? *Well, Caroline went, but I would not.*

That Sunday, after the service, I asked Caroline how it had gone. She casually said that it was good and, by the way, she had been *born again!*

I wasn't familiar with the term since it was not used in the denomination we had grown up in, but it sounded contradictory and even vaguely sinister and cultish to me. How can one be born again? I asked her why in the world she would do such a thing.

She had a simple answer: "I felt the presence of GOD!"

"Well," I said, "that's new." I asked whether I could go the following week. I did. I sensed God's presence, gave my life to Jesus and was born again!

As part of a lineage of samurai warriors stretching back for hundreds of years, I say that I did what every red-blooded samurai would do: I followed my wife into the kingdom of God!

Roy advised us to go *all in*. This meant attending church, praying, reading the Bible, and tithing. So we did!

Three months passed and all was going well, except for believing the Bible literally! I had the toughest time accepting the Word as truth. How could it be, the Bible having been assembled from many sources with portions written over a vast period of time in numerous languages finally translated to English? My high-minded Ivy League education fought the idea of taking anything literally, much less something with such a mixed pedigree.

I've since come to understand what taking the Bible *literally* means. One must truly understand what is being said by looking at the context, studying the original text, and understanding whether the passage is meant prophetically, poetically, historically, allegorically, etc.

While you might not jump through all these hoops for every word, it's a very good thing to do for significant passages. When this is done and the true meaning of the text is understood, then it must be taken for what it says, not twisted to fit one's world view. This is what I've learned to be taking the Word of God literally.

Seeing

I didn't understand this while on the freeway as I mulled over the scripture I'd just read that morning.

> "Bring the whole tithe into the storehouse, that there may be food in my house. Test me in this," says the Lord Almighty, "and see if I will not throw open the floodgates of heaven and pour out so much blessing that there will not be room enough to store it." (Malachi 3:10, NIV)

Well, okay, I thought, *we've been tithing for three months, and while we have enough, it's not like this word describes, "Open the floodgates of heaven and pour out so much blessing that there will not be room enough to store it."* I tend to be very practical.

At just that second, three thoughts came into my mind: (1) *This will happen through large projects.* (2) *You will be prepared to do them.* (3) *Then a specific figure, twenty times the size of any project we had done, came to mind. I had never specifically heard from God before!*

Nevertheless, as a zealous convert, I rushed into our small office and gathered the six others—all non-Christians—and told them what *God had just told me!* I saw them back off, some with eyes like saucers, and I imagined them thinking, *Francis has really flipped out. Maybe I should find a job at another office!* This was Monday.

Maui Marriott

On Friday, three gentlemen I knew came into the office at noon without an appointment. Everyone else was out to lunch, so I ushered them into the conference room and we talked. They explained that they wanted us to work on a large 720-room hotel project. I thought that this was nice, but the catch 22 of hotels is that you don't get to design one unless you already designed one. *We had not!*

Understand, there's a lot of talk about projects before one truly materializes. It takes so much money, a site, a market, and a willing client to make a building feasible. Even small buildings cost millions of dollars, and it's almost a miracle when a larger building is developed!

Given all this, I was not taking the conversation very seriously. That is, until one of the men gave the budget for the project! *It was exactly the number that God had given me!*

Caught totally unaware, I felt faint! I drew everything I had of my professional composure to whisper, "That's interesting." There was one condition: we had to have a set of conceptual drawings submitted to Marriott headquarters in DC in six weeks. This is something that normally takes months!

By the time the men left, the others had returned to the office. I gathered them together and gave them the news! We were all excited and young enough to not know what we didn't know. There was no way we could design such a huge and specific project, along one of the most beautiful beaches on Maui, without experience...but for God!

We immediately called one of our partners who had taken a sabbatical to teach architecture at the University of Hawaii and told him to go to the library and borrow every book on hotels that he could find. We were going to do a charette (a focused design session) on Saturday, and we wanted to be prepared.

Marriott Kaanapali Beach Hotel

Marriott Kaanapali Beach Hotel

First Vision

That night, as I prayed, God gave me a vision for the project. This is the first time I experienced envisioning with God! Prior to this, I had developed a practice of dreaming designs. It was based on what I had been taught in school, that the designs were *in you* and what was needed was to get them out. This, for me, had entailed a couple weeks of barely speaking to others and being in deep concentration until a dream came. *When I dreamed it, I could quickly sketch it.*

The process had *worked!* It produced designs that won national and international awards. It even allowed us to win a national AIA Honor Award for the design of a church in Chico, California. I was only twenty-seven years old!

I had, however, developed a pain in my stomach, night blindness, and my hair began turning white. I was not well, so I went for a medical checkup. The doctor asked me what I was doing, and after I told him, he said, "Whatever it is, stop! You're killing yourself!" I was in a bind, though, because I didn't know another way to design quality buildings.

After God provided the design of the Marriott Hotel, however, I realized that the source of the creative vision was not me, but God! All I had to do was be a faithful vessel to receive his inspiration! The pain stopped, my night vision was healed, and my hair turned black again.

God's Design

The Lord not only showed me the design of the Marriott Hotel, but also gave me poetry and images of cultural objects we were to include in the design folio. We gathered the following morning, discussed the project, worked at our drafting boards for several hours, then regrouped and put our design sketches on the wall for critique. *Everyone liked God's design!*

These were precomputer days. All our presentation drawings were done in ink on vellum or board! It's difficult to imagine today, but we hand-drew everything with pens and assembled a bound folio of our drawings with text and cultural images. Off it went to Marriott headquarters with us following two weeks later.

At Marriott, I found myself in the largest conference room I had been in up to that time and since. We were seated at the longest conference table that I'd ever seen. In addition, all the seats at the table, and the chairs along the wall, were filled.

At one end of the table was Bill Marriott Jr., looking through our folio. A person named Jack stood and spoke, "I head the A&C Section (architecture and construction) with 210 people, and I don't understand what Mr. Oda is doing here because we design all Marriott's hotels. We know what's needed and our name is on the building!"

I thought to myself, *We have seven people.*

Immediately, Don Graham, the dean of developers in Hawaii, who had done the Ala Moana Center—the largest center in the US at that time—stood and said, "The reason Mr. Oda is here is that we want to have a Hawaiian resort hotel." (Until this time, Marriott had not operated a resort hotel, and its properties were either business and airport hotels or motels.) "In any case," Don then said with authority, "Mr. Oda is an expert in hotels!"

I was shocked! What was I doing here?

Yet even in my moment of doubt, the Lord spoke, "I told you that you'd be here. Didn't I give you the number?"

As Don sat down, Mr. Marriott spoke, "Ladies and gentlemen, I like this. We'll do it!" And that was that!

In this short period of my early Christian experience, I learned that God speaks to us, he cares about business, and he shows us practical visions. Who knew?

God's Visions

Much later, I saw a passage that perfectly describes what I had experienced. King David, describing to Solomon what God had shown him regarding the Temple, says, "All this, the Lord made me understand in writing, by His hand upon me, all the works of these plans" (2 Chronicles 28:19, NKJV).

This experience was also confirmed by no less than C. S. Lewis. He wrote, "Some people seem to think that I began by asking myself how I could say something about Christianity to children, then fixed on the fairy tale as an instrument, then collected information about child psychology;...then drew up a list of basic Christian truths and hammered out allegories to embody them. This is pure moonshine. I couldn't write this way. All my seven Narnian books began with seeing pictures in my head."

Working with God's Visions

Lewis continues: "*The Lion, the Witch, and the Wardrobe* began with a picture of a Faun carrying an umbrella and parcels in a snowy wood… Then one day… I said to myself: 'Let's try to make a story about it.' At first, I had very little idea how the story would go. But then suddenly Aslan came bounding into it…once he was there, He pulled the whole story together."

Unlike David's completely detailed vision of the Temple, Lewis' description is of a progressive vision, inspired at different points. The practice of daily envisioning includes both realities. It's often the case, however, that even detailed visions need development and further work. The key to the progressive vision is not to dismiss its initial form as meaningless and silly, like "a Faun carrying an umbrella and parcels in a snowy wood." At the same time, you shouldn't take a detailed vision as complete, unless the Lord says so. With practice, you'll recognize the difference and may nurture visions from embryonic stages to classics like *The Lion, the Witch, and the Wardrobe!* It just takes practice!

CHAPTER 2

GOD'S FAITH

*Now faith is the substance of things hoped
for, the evidence of things not seen.*
—Hebrews 11:1 (KJV)

Visioning for Life

This began my life-long practice of envisioning with God. I start every day by reading Scripture before prayer envisioning. I use a simple Bible study as a guide. I meditate and journal what I feel the Lord is showing me about his Word.

I then read my journaled prayers and vision from the day before. I record in caps, AMEN or ANSWERED to the prayers. I then start the prayers for the day. These I journal.

After my time of prayer, I envision for the day. Many morning visions relate to my morning prayers. In order to do this, I consciously try to "empty" my mind of thoughts and concerns, even the focused thoughts which directed my prayers. I sometimes ask the Lord to show me something about a concern I have as a form of directed envisioning. I prefer, however, to "empty" my mind so that I can be a clean vessel to receive whatever the Lord has for me.

As I receive visions, I simply record them on my iPad since I can type much faster than I can write. I simply observe and record these visions. I do not put any of my impressions on what the Lord has for me. It's only on the following day, when I review the visions of the prior day, that I ask the Lord for discernment as to the meaning of the visions. *All of this takes a minimum of an hour a day, every day.*

I've found that the process of "emptying" my mind has several residual benefits. For one, it eliminates the chatter that might be in my mind. I call this *monkey-mind.* Over time, this practice has allowed peace to reign in my mind to receive visions more clearly and cleanly. This peace and clarity tends to remain with me throughout the day, and it would be difficult, if not impossible, for me to go through a day without beginning in this way. *Doing this daily for decades changes your life!*

Another huge benefit is that I have discovered that few things are as they initially seem. The emptying of my mind has trained me to not allow pre-judgements or prejudices regarding people, situations, institutions, opportunities, or problems to color my reception of God's vision. *The truth becomes more apparent beginning with an emptied mind.*

In addition, an emptied mind doesn't recognize the normal pressures and stresses of circumstances.

Whether something is possible or not is not a concern. Whether it's something I can do or not is inconsequential to an emptied mind. Whether something is feasible or not doesn't color one's reception. There's no fear in an emptied mind. With an emptied mind, one is free.

I'll address this issue again, but I don't want to confuse this with Zen or other types of meditation which generally focus on eliminating all forms of thought from one's mind, even the thought of not having any thoughts. The emptied mind I'm describing is always aware of God's presence, whether the Father, Son, or Holy Spirit. *Therefore, while the mind is emptied of the cares of the world, it is filled with the presence of God.*

The way I empty my mind, a practice in many disciplines including mindfulness training, I recognize random thoughts and impressions. Trying to dismiss thoughts is, in fact, focusing your attention on them. It's a fruitless process. It's best to simply recognize the thought and then put it aside. I find it helpful to envision a shelf, and not a trash basket, because the shelf allows me to come back to the thought or issue after I receive direction from the Lord. Once on the shelf, I'm not tempted to revisit the thought, but know that it's there for future reference.

I record in my journal exactly what I'm seeing or hearing without embellishment. This is important so as not to slant God's vision. I try to be as objective as possible. I also don't try to interpret a vision the day I journal it. I review it the following day or over a number of days.

This process allows me to be more objective in interpretation. It's of no value if I slant a vision to my purposes.

It's important to know that some visions are fragments. They don't make sense alone but are pieces of a puzzle and need to be combined with other subsequent visions to make a whole picture. The review of journaled visions allows this kind of realization. I have learned to be patient in discerning what God's showing me rather than jumping to false conclusions.

Some of the visions are significant, yet most are everyday things. I've found that it doesn't matter since the process is like working out physically. When you work out, you don't pick the heaviest weights but light ones so you can do a lot of reps to build and strengthen your muscles. Visioning is similar and builds *spiritual muscles.*

Spiritual muscles need to be strong, toned, and have the capacity to receive God's messages. Too often, I believe, people call out to God but can't hold on to his answers. This is because they usually call out at a time of great need. A big answer comes, yet they don't have the spiritual muscles to hold on to the answer. Answers drop to the ground because they seem impossible, and are dismissed!

So, strengthening spiritual muscles daily is a must. It's like working out daily to win the race that the Apostle Paul alludes to in 1 Corinthians 9:25, "Everyone who competes in the games goes into strict training. They do it to get a crown that will not last, but we do it to get a crown that will last forever."

Envisioning Builds Faith

In my years as a pastor, I found that many people don't know what they're hoping for. They say "shotgun" prayers, hoping that they'll hit something. Daily envisioning shows what you are hoping for!

While envisioning, what you hope for becomes apparent. Once you see something clearly in the spiritual realm, it is easy, with faith, to have absolute certainty that it will come to pass. In fact, that measure of faith given to everyone referred to in Romans 12:3 is more than enough to bridge the gap.

This is what we architects do as a matter of course. We envision projects and draw them with our computers. Once a project is defined and all the technical drawings are done, the building is as much as finished in our minds. We can describe every part of it in detail. While not yet seen in the physical, it is very real in the conceptual. *Its actual construction is almost just an artifact of its conception!*

Practice One Thousand Times

You might be tempted to assume that, as an architect, I have a special gift in envisioning that you might not possess. This may be true to an extent, but I can guarantee you that if you practice envisioning daily, you'll be as adept at it as I have become. It's not a matter of gifting but of practice!

My favorite Zen saying is "Practice a thousand times, then abandon yourself to inspiration."

Bruce Lee said, "Don't fear the man who has practiced one thousand moves one time, but fear the man who has practiced one move one thousand times."

A pastor friend, R. K. Castillo, is really into jujitsu. He practices five days a week and sometimes two or three times in a day. He took Bruce Lee's saying to heart and practiced only one move every session for a whole year. This worked so well that he's now on his tenth year practicing this one move! Why? It works! He consistently defeats higher black belts!

Like Pastor R. K., you can master this one move of envisioning! It just means practicing it at least one thousand times. Before you get discouraged, let me give you a little science that will tell you why this practice is important.

Research in neuroscience has recently discovered that God's design for our brains allows us to continually learn. This is called "neuroplasticity." It's good news for us all!

What is fascinating is that as we use the same connections between neurons in our brains repeatedly (one thousand times), these pathways are strengthened. As these pathways are strengthened, the connections become thick, hardy road maps that link parts of the brain to do certain things very well. We see this all the time in athletics, language, music, and in any activity that requires repetition and practice. This is the way we learned to read, do math, dance.

Neurologist Judy Willis says, "Practice makes permanent." *The more times the network is stimulated, the stronger and more efficient it becomes.*

When first learning to read or do math, it's a challenge because the networks are not set in our brains. As we practice, however, it becomes easier and easier. This is the way it is with envisioning. At first, you may not get much or you don't know whether what you are getting is from God. But after a while, you begin to associate the voice that you hear or the sense that you have to things that come to pass. You also recognize when things don't work. *You begin to recognize the voice of God.*

I like to see pictures. My wife Caroline, who is an educator and an English major, more often gets words. Normally, it's a combination of both.

Daily envisioning and journaling is also like tuning a radio daily. Even if reception is perfect one day, the dial may need adjustment the following day. I think we often go off frequency because of the busyness of life. *Daily tuning is essential to be on God's frequency!*

God's Voice

Scripture says that the sheep know the shepherd's voice. Yet, as I noted, I have found that the greatest challenge many Christians have is that they don't recognize the shepherd's voice. As you become familiar with God's voice and receive his plans and purposes, you will become so confident that you'll come to stake your life on what you envision!

Many years ago, after Caroline and I had completed our morning prayers, I turned to her and said, "God just told me to change the educational system for architects in the United States."

She turned to me and said, "That's nice."

This assignment was the furthest thing from my mind, but it was definitely the voice of God that I had heard. In fact, one way I have come to identify the voice of God is that he so often tells me to do things I don't want to do, don't know how to do, things that seem impossible to do. I've come to realize that my feelings and sense of what's possible have to align with God, not the other way around. Also, being able or qualified to do something has nothing to do with it! Was Moses qualified? As Ed Silvoso teaches, what matters is being *chosen* which carries the power, ability, and resources to accomplish whatever God desires.

I immediately went to Elmer Botsai, who was dean of the school of architecture at the University of Hawaii. I explained the assignment God had given me. Elmer said that if I chaired the committee of practitioners and academics who would develop the program, he would support the concept of a program toward a doctor of architecture degree for all architects!

I happened to be on the advisory board of the school of architecture of Cornell University, my alma mater. I made a presentation to the board at a meeting in San Francisco, thinking that a private school in the east and a public school in the west would pretty much cause the nation to change. *The Cornell group rejected the idea.* So I began to work with the committee in Hawaii. It took seven and a half years to develop the program with the complexities of a new curriculum and transitioning from the existing program.

After that time, we presented to the architecture faculty and the faculty senate of the university. The proposal failed at both levels! Yet God had mandated this, and I knew that I had heard his voice!

So, when a new dean soon thereafter arrived on campus, I went to him with the proposal. He said that he would support it, but that I had to chair the committee. After another seven and a half years, a total of fifteen years, we again made our proposal. I had learned something from the first time, so I asked the dean to just get the approval of his faculty, which he did.

I then approached the chair of the faculty senate. He was a distinguished geophysicist from New Zealand who was on a committee that I chaired for twelve years composed of business leaders and the leaders of the university including the president, chancellor, and the chair of the academic senate.

After explaining the program, the faculty senate chair said that it sounded very good.

I responded, "But you don't understand. The last time it went before your group, it was rejected."

He said, "Francis, you don't understand! I pick the committee!"

I sheepishly thanked him, and it was approved! I then took the proposal to the president.

For many years, Caroline and I had gone to an annual retreat of thought-leaders from the community always held at a resort hotel. Internationally prominent speakers would come and discuss issues with us. We ran across the president and his wife having lunch at the retreat that year and they invited us to join them. As Caroline got into a conversation with the president's wife, I made a pitch for the program to the president! It must have been a great hamburger he was eating because he was totally focused on it. He didn't want to make eye contact until I said that we had done a business plan for the program, and he might not have to spend another dime in the school of architecture because the program would attract students from around the world!

He immediately looked up and said, "Why didn't you say so at the beginning? Approved!"

The final step was the board of regents. Its chair happened to be my PR person. I called her, and she said not to worry. The program was passed in 1999 and initiated in 2000. *It is now being discussed as the model for all architectural education in the United States!*

It took another three years to get the approval of the national boards which certify architects. We received the approvals. In all, we had spent eighteen years in the process.

I doubt that anyone would have faulted me for saying, after the first seven and a half years, that we gave it a good try. Yet I knew that God had mandated this because I recognized his voice. I knew, therefore, that it would come to pass. Knowing the shepherd's voice changes your life!

CHAPTER 3

GOD'S OPPORTUNITIES

*But you are a chosen people, a royal priesthood, a holy nation,
God's special possession, that you may declare the praises of him
who called you out of darkness into his wonderful light.*
—1 Peter 2:9 (NIV)

Marketplace Ministry

It was recognizing the voice of God that changed my life and caused the opportunity for me to become a pastor. At first, I certainly didn't see it as an opportunity.

Victor Borgia, our beloved pastor, died suddenly. He had just been diagnosed with pancreatic cancer, and within weeks, he went to be with the Lord. Caroline and I were helping Victor to plant a church related to the then largest church in Hawaii. *We were devastated!*

As a member of the board, I sat with others to determine our course of action. We thought we had three choices: (1) Call a group of potential candidates to speak at the church, then select one as our pastor; (2) join an existing church body; and (3) disband the church. We felt that the third alternative was not responsible, so we went forward with the first two.

We met with several pastors of existing churches and always found a problem. We were Pentecostals, and many good churches were not. We did not want to join a denomination. We could not find a good fit. We were also in a quandary about interviewing and listening to potential pastors. We knew that everyone who's been in ministry for any period of time has a dynamite sermon. While we could have a string of candidates come and give their dynamite sermons, we'd be very impressed but still not know who to pick.

To help us through this, we asked Dr. Sam Sasser, who had been senior pastor of our *mother* church, to assist us. Sam and his wife, Flo, were dear friends, now living on the mainland. Sam was writing a book and loved the idea of finishing it in Hawaii!

We spent thirteen weeks studying the scripture and praying. Finally, Sam and I sensed that the Lord was saying that he'd pick our future leaders from among us. We further discerned that four of us were chosen. Our response was, *"But we work!"* We four agreed to spend two weeks in prayer and fasting. I spoke to Caroline and my children about this.

I also spoke to my partners. I said that if God called me, I'd be gone from the firm in two weeks! They almost fell on the floor! At that time in the practice, as president and CEO, I was responsible for bringing in the majority of clients and projects. My partners could see a threat to the practice itself.

Called

So we prayed and fasted.

During the two weeks, the Lord spoke to me very specifically. I had thought that being called to the ministry meant leaving the marketplace and going to the four walls of a church. Like most Christians, this was the only model I knew. He told me to follow *Paul's model.*

Paul left the synagogue and went to the marketplace to teach and preach. He ministered in the marketplace and famously in Acts 20:33–34. "I have not coveted anyone's silver or gold or clothing. You yourselves know that these hands of mine have supplied my own needs and the needs of my companions." God revealed this other pattern of ministry to me—the marketplace ministry!

After the Lord confirmed my call and the call of the others, I went to my family and partners and said that while I was going to be in *full-time ministry*, that full time would be in the church and in the marketplace. I'd since realized that God never calls us to part-time anything! He doesn't say, "You can minister on your days off or on weekends when you have the time." No, he requires all of us, all the time, in every venue! He calls all of us to full-time ministry!

I've been asked many times how I can operate with this *dual* ministry or *tentmaking* ministry. It's clear to me that this is one ministry. It's just in multiple settings. We all have multiple roles, such as husband/wife, son/daughter, parent/child, worker/boss, player/coach. We can go from one role to the other seamlessly and without a second thought. Should it be so hard in the church? It's not God's plan.

Scripture is very strongly *one* oriented, as in the Lord being *three-in-one* as Jesus was saying in John 10:30, "I and the Father are one," and in John 17:22–23, "I have given them the glory that you gave me, that they may be one as we are one—I in them and you in me—so that they may be brought to complete unity."

The label "tentmaking" in the modern church often carries a pejorative implication. Tentmaking pastors are thought to be rather unsuccessful so they must moonlight. Yet the term comes from Paul, and he's our model of a pastor and apostle, especially for gentiles. He's the writer of much of the New Testament and he planted many of the early churches in the non-Jewish world. Tentmaking should be a badge of honor!

We need to overcome the schizophrenia of the Christian world. God did not make the home, business and church as separate worlds, yet we act in one way at home, another at work and a third way at Church. We even have different vocabularies in each venue. I believe that the Lord wants us to be one in ourselves, as well as in him. *I, therefore, act the same in the boardroom as I do in church as I do at home.* It's too stressful to do it any other way.

New Life Church Honolulu

With the vision of marketplace ministry, we began our effort to reestablish the ministry that became New Life Church Honolulu.

During this time of fasting and prayer, the Lord also gave me five visionary principles:

1. We were to base the ministry on the Word of God and the power of his Holy Spirit.
2. We were to be marketplace ministers. This meant that everyone was to be a minister in the marketplace (have a job that allowed self-support), as well as a minister in the church.
3. Women were to be co-leaders in the ministry. Two of the original four selected were anointed women.
4. We should speak with an indigenous voice. This meant we should honor the host Hawaiian culture. In our work in Japan, the Philippines, Tahiti, Indonesia, and elsewhere, we honor the cultures within which we minister.
5. We were not to be a large ocean liner, like the church we came from, but a fleet of canoes. On an ocean liner, 20 percent of the people (crew) do all the work, while 80 percent are passengers, expecting to be served, fed, and burped. On a canoe, everyone is crew, knows each other, and works together. As we reached 300 members, we were to start a new canoe with one hundred people and a new captain (senior pastor). We would multiply in this way. These canoes would have all the benefits of interpersonal ministry and, as part of a fleet, would do larger works.

These principles, which we've followed to this day, came more as prophetic words than visions. This points to the relationship among visions, dreams, and prophecy. In their very nature, visions are prophetic. They usually show things to come. Dreams may also be prophetic and visionary. My use of the term *envision with God*, therefore, does not apply only to seeing but also hearing God's prophetic words, sensing the move of his Holy Spirit and having dreams. *The point is not the medium but having a clear and consistent connection to the message sender!*

We see in Joel 2:28–29,

> And afterward, I will pour out my Spirit on all people. Your sons and daughters will prophesy, your old men will dream dreams, your young men will see visions. Even on my servants, both men and women, I will pour out my Spirit in those days.

I believe those days are today!

After the confirmation of our calling (opportunity) and our discerning the unique manner of our ministry, we were ordained by Dr. Sam Sasser and launched into ministry. We immediately encountered headwinds. Some people thought we were starting a cult because of our marketplace focus which, at that time, was not familiar in the Christian world. We were also challenged regarding having women in leadership positions. We were told that this was not scriptural, a contention that's addressed in Ed Silvoso's book *Women: God's Secret Weapon* and Loren Cunningham's *Why Not Women?* This we learned later when we came to know these men well. At that time, we felt like orphans.

At the beginning, our church met in homes, hotel conference rooms, and a school cafetorium.

Finally, we found refuge in the sanctuary of St. Mary's Episcopal Church. Their pastor and congregation warmly welcomed us to use their facilities after their services. We spent several years in their hospitable environment working out the visions that God had given us.

Chinatown

One day, as I was walking through the lobby of a downtown office building, a Christian realtor friend called out to me and asked if I knew that a church a few blocks away on the edge of Chinatown was for sale. It was a converted old theater and the church that owned it was building a campus in Central Oahu. I asked him to arrange for me to look at the property.

The next day, after a walk-through with a good friend, Apostle Emanuele Cannistraci, I knew the theater fit God's vision that I'd received that morning! I said, "We'll buy it!" I then worked with the board to figure out how!

Together, our tiny congregation of thirty-four adults and God worked out a plan that aligned with God's vision! We bought the property! The decision was made before the plan as to how to purchase and whether we could *afford* to purchase was developed. This is how the principle of "believing is seeing" applies. The vision determined the belief. The group's plan to buy supported the individual vision.

As the head of a major business in Hawaii, I can understand that this might seem irresponsible. I should have gotten the approval of the board before announcing the decision! We should have thoroughly analyzed the pros and cons, and looked at the economic implications before acting. Yet had we done this, we probably would have backed away from the million-dollar purchase. After all, we were only thirty-four adults!

In fact, I got the approval of the board before the formal purchase offer was made, but not before the decision to buy was made! See the difference? If our analysis rather than God's vision had determined our decision, our congregation might not have multiplied many times since, and our ministry might not have reached nations! This was fifteen years ago. The building is located on the corner of one of the gateways to downtown Honolulu. It's also at the edge of Chinatown which was plagued with crime, homelessness, and substance abuse—perfect for the work of Christ!

We prayer-walked the neighborhood for the months before we moved in. We continue to do so today. We pray for the Chinese merchants and for their businesses and families. We pray for the homeless. People were healed on the streets!

One story sticks out. Dr. Charles Gregory, one of our team leaders, went into a Chinese woman's shop and asked if she wanted prayer. She told him to buy something or get out and threw the pamphlet that he'd given her on the floor! The next week, Charles went back! The shop owner's jaw dropped, and she thought he was an idiot! Didn't he understand her the first time? Well, Charles and his team persisted, often bringing food gifts like Chinese buns with sweet pork (*manapua*). Finally, this woman asked for prayer for her son. Months later, she gave her life to the Lord!

One morning, as we were collecting the offering, Charles came up to the platform with a fist full of crumpled dollar bills. He asked whether he should put them in the offering plate. I asked what the problem was. He said that the team had gone into one of the two bars in Chinatown that were open on Sunday morning to pray for the people. The people at the bar took an offering. The team tried not to take the money, but the people insisted!

"Well," I said to Charles, "they want to offer it to the Lord, so who are we to judge it?"

A week later, the woman who owned the bar sent a check for $1,000 to the church, something she's done again from time to time since.

Chinatown has changed a lot since we first arrived fifteen years ago. Through the efforts and prayers of several churches, the work of civic groups and the government, Chinatown has become a place of cool restaurants, art galleries, and fashion boutiques. It's become a happening place where drug deals that were so apparent and universal on the streets and back alleys are not so evident. Crime is down, as is homelessness. It's not that all the problems are gone. Chinatown, however, is now a place where families of all races can raise children, live, work, and play.

Caroline and I are now apostles of the church and of Transform Our World. The senior pastor of New Life Church is now Jocelyn McMahon, who served as executive pastor for many years. She's a woman of vision ably assisted in ministry by a team of pastors, including Maria Holstein, Jacob Chung, Barbara Gatewood, and Dennis Yokota. Ministers include Alan Snell, Rosemary Yokota, Tim Nishida and Travis Nishida.

CHAPTER 4

GOD'S RIGHT PEOPLE

The Lord said to Gideon, "With the three hundred men
that lapped I will save you and give the Midianites
into your hands. Let all of the others go home."
—Judges 7:7

G70

Since the prophetic word I received on the freeway, God has blessed our practice. Every part of that word has been fulfilled. We have done major projects throughout the Pacific and even in Africa.

The second portion of the prophecy—that we would be prepared—is a story of its own. Since we were a small seven-person office, we did not have the technical firepower and knowledge to put together a major complex like a 720-room resort hotel. On top of that, it was a very busy time in Hawaii's economy. There was no one available to hire.

One day, my partner Gus Ishihara received a call from a person named Johnny. He was well known in the profession as a very gifted technical person but also as a con artist and a womanizer. He asked to speak to us about a job. While I didn't know Johnny personally, I knew his reputation. I felt that he couldn't work at Group 70. Gus said that we should at least speak to him, so we had lunch.

During the lunch, noticing that I was detached from the conversation, Johnny looked at me directly and said, "Francis, I know what you're thinking, but can I tell you a story?"

I said, "Sure."

Johnny told us that two years earlier he'd had a heart attack. This we knew, but what we didn't know was that he called out to God and promised that he would change his life if he was spared! Looking straight at me, Johnny said that he was a new man, not the one I thought he was. I said, "Based on that, I'm willing to have you come to the firm."

Johnny was the right person for the job! He was so respected by other technical draftsmen that he was able to draw six people to the firm who just wanted to work with him!

This team of seven, augmented by a few of those already in the firm, produced the construction drawings for the Marriott Kaanapali Hotel in record time.

Johnny also turned out to be one of the most trustworthy and beloved people in our firm. He was sixty when the Marriott project began, and he retired at sixty-five after its completion. During those five years, in addition to completing the hotel, he restored relationships with an ex-wife and his children. Banished from his first family, he reconciled with them and everyone else who he had hurt. Shortly after his retirement, Johnny suffered a second heart attack and died!

At the funeral, his wife came to me very excited. She asked if I knew where Johnny was being buried.

Confused, I said, "I thought it was here."

She said, "Yes, yes, but where?"

Now I was really confused! She took my hand and led me to a columbarium close to the chapel.

"Here!" she said. Her excitement was that the name of the crypt area of Johnny's internment was the Lokelani Court.

The lokelani is the Maui rose. This is the symbol of the Marriott Kaanapali Hotel!

A huge three-dimensional logo of the Maui rose is on the side of the hotel! It was God's sign to us that he had taken Johnny only after he had a chance to set his life in order and was at peace with God and man. We rejoiced!

MAUI MARRIOTT HOTEL AT KAʻANAPALI
MAUI, HAWAIʻI

Dr. Ed Silvoso, TOW

The blend of pulpit and marketplace ministry was still rather unusual in the Christian community and certainly in the market-place. We were outliers both at New Life Church and G70. One day in 2003, Charles Kaneshiro, then one of our young architects and now the President and COO of G70, asked me to be his guest at a luncheon sponsored by his church. The guest speaker was a fellow named Ed Silvoso. At the time, I had neither heard of Ed nor read any of his books.

At the talk, however, he spoke directly to my spirit! Ed addressed marketplace ministry and had written about it in his book *Anointed For Business*. He pointed out that the heart of communities was no longer the church but the marketplace. In order to transform a community, therefore, one had to transform its marketplace! Wow, this confirmed God's calling in our ministry!

Then a strange thing happened at the meeting's end. The pastor of Charles' church, Cal Chinen, who I didn't know, called on me to give the final prayer. I did so in full Pentecostal voice! Ed immediately came up to me and a life-long bond was established. I had found a soul-mate!

Ed invited Caroline and me to the global conference of Harvest Evangelism to be held in Argentina, but we could not attend that year. Ed said that the conference would change our lives, but how many times had I heard that before? However, we went to the conference the next year, and our lives have never been the same!

We learned the principles of Ed's seminal book on marketplace ministry, *Anointed for Business*. We read the other books he had written up to that time: *That None Should Perish, Prayer Evangelism,* and *Women: God's Secret Weapon*. These books affirmed the words and visions that the Lord had given us concerning marketplace ministry, women as co-leaders in the kingdom, and gave us much, much more. More than anything, we were no longer orphans but part of a global family with the same calling and vision. We had found our family!

A significant part of Ed's teaching is the need to focus on transformation in our spheres of influence. We learned that it isn't enough to simply be ministers in the marketplace, occasionally praying for fellow workers and being good Christians. We had to bring the kingdom of God to the marketplace, which means the transformational presence of God!

Transform Our World (TOW)

Thousands have gathered to reaffirm this truth and give testimony to their experiences. This has emerged as Transform Our World (TOW).

Ed Silvoso is CEO of both Harvest Evangelism (HE, the parent organization) and TOW. Ray Pinson, a visionary tech entrepreneur, chairs the HE board; I chair TOW.

When asked to chair TOW, I refused three times! I felt I was unqualified. I argued that there were people with much larger companies in the movement, much larger churches, and besides, I was in the middle of the Pacific. All true, but Ed and the Holy Spirit kept after me.

Finally, Caroline told me, "The Lord's put this into your hands. Grasp it!"

I did. Thank God for wives!

Through TOW, the Lord has opened new opportunities for all of us to disciple and transform nations with the right people! Pastors, as well as leaders in business, education and government—who all began with traditional ideas of ministry—have adopted the paradigm of discipling communities and nations.

Two pastors of the movement are Brian and Margaret Burton, from Thailand. They had ministered as missionaries from the UK in Thailand for sixteen years and shepherded a church of less than fifty people. While this is a large Christian church in the South of Thailand, it's not at all what they had expected.

Although they never felt defeated, the Burtons were searching for a better way. In 2007, Brian attended one of Harvest Evangelism's global conferences in Argentina with one of his church elders, Heidi Gempel, and then went to a regional conference in Hawaii to hear more. Margaret wasn't able to join him because her passport had less than six months on it and she wouldn't be allowed back into Thailand if she were to travel. Brian had read *Anointed for Business* a few years earlier, and hearing Ed's teaching in person verified to him that what they had been doing was a biblical approach and he wasn't straying from his calling as a pastor.

Inspired by what he'd heard in Argentina, Brian returned to Thailand and declared that he was the pastor of Phuket and his people were marketplace ministers! The church became even more involved with efforts that served the entire community.

One project they took on in 2005 was rebuilding a school that had been wiped out by the infamous Banda Aceh tsunami. Brian felt led by the Spirit to compete against large Asian corporations to rebuild the school, even with no money and no influence. The corporations had promised to plan, build, and pay for the school!

Brian, however, had God's vision. The king of Thailand liked Brian's vision and submittal and selected it. While the king supplied the Royal Thai Engineers, Brian raised over one million US dollars from 32 nations to build the school and equip it, thanks in part to daily televised reports in the UK by the BBC's competitor, ITV!

Brian and Margaret have also worked with the governor of Phuket, the chief of police, and other government and community leaders. Their church also ministers to marginalized Burmese refugees and other minorities. This once small church, today numbers into the thousands and is distributed over several cities. Brian and Margaret, as well as their team, now minister to Phuket, other provinces, and the nation.

Pastor Poncho Murguia is another wonderful example. He had a thriving church in Ciudad Juárez, Mexico, with a campus that also included a Bible school.

One day, after decades of ministry, the Lord told him to give the church and facility to his leaders and to pitch a tent in a specific park and await further instructions. Poncho had a hard time accepting this and argued with the Lord. This was his family! After all, he had baptized and married many who were now parents themselves. How could he leave them? Poncho was especially concerned about how his wife, Gelus, would take this. He asked the Lord to spare her the anguish.

One day, he finally was prepared to accept the Lord's direction and present it to Gelus. He told her to sit down. He related what God had said, and she began to cry.

Oh no, Poncho thought, *This is going to be bad!*

Gelus looked at him and told him that the Lord ha[c]
this three years earlier! She was waiting for Poncho to g[e]
Why does the Holy Spirit always seem to speak to and throug[
first?

Well, after turning the church over to his elders, Po..cno sat
under his tent. After a few days, a newspaper reporter came to him
and asked what he was protesting. He said he wasn't protesting anything but talking to God.

So the reporter asked, "What's God saying?"

The reporter went back to his editor and told him about
Poncho. The editor assigned the reporter to go to the park daily to
find out what God was saying! Soon a TV crew appeared and daily
asked Poncho what God was saying to him. Many began to come out
to pray and accompany Poncho in his vigil. At the end of the 21-day
fast, four thousand people gathered at the park to close the fast with
Poncho!

The visions and direction that Poncho received have taken him
along a unique and incredible path. He first led the cleansing of the
Juárez prison, the center of criminal and drug activities in the city.
He then led the development of one of the best children's muse-
ums in the world, La Rodadora, which is now affiliated with the
Smithsonian. The Lord showed him to do this as a version of Sunday
School in the twenty-first century!

He subsequently was moved to adopt sicarios, who are cartel hitmen. A member of Poncho's church had been a cellmate of a sicario
who was a leader of several teams of hitmen. Both had received the
Lord in prison, but after being released, the sicario went back to his
old life.

One day, the Lord told the member of Poncho's church to find
his old cellmate to tell him that God loves him and he was to leave
his life of crime and return to the Lord. All he knew was the town
where his friend was reported to be, so he went there. This might
have been foolhardy since one doesn't just go around asking about
a senior cartel leader. In obedience, however, the fellow went to the
town and asked the first person he saw about the whereabouts of his
old cellmate.

The response was, "Who wants to know?"

God's messenger explained his relationship with the cartel boss and what God had told him to say.

The person responded, "I'll take you to him. I'm his brother."

They went to a home on a corner and the brother said to wait outside. He went in and came out with the boss, and after asking him if he could pray for him, he said to walk to a more private place since his teams were inside planning their hits. They went to a far corner of the block. As they spoke, a car quickly pulled up to the house they had just left, men jumped out, sprayed the building with bullets, killing everybody that was inside, then jumped into their car and sped off!

In shock, the sicario leader realized that God had spared him. Convinced that he needed to obey the Lord, he went to his bosses to do the impossible, leave the cartel. After telling them the story, they surprisingly allowed him to leave, but gave him a warning. He could never return to the *business* in any way, or he and his family would be annihilated!

In the meantime, the Lord was speaking to Poncho about adopting sicarios. The Lord said that these hitmen also need families, God's family. He shared with the Lord his concern that this could put his congregation in jeopardy since if an opposing gang wanted to hit someone, they might indiscriminately break into a service and spray everyone with deadly gunfire. This was their MO.

Poncho's associate came to him with the ex-sicario and asked if his friend could come to a service. Knowing what the Lord had said, but wanting to protect his people, Poncho asked to delay for a week. At the next service, Poncho shared what God had said about sicarios with his congregation. He offered to place everyone who wanted to leave in another good church, with his blessings. He encouraged them to think about their families and themselves.

The next week, Poncho had no idea how many people would be at the service. To his surprise, he saw that everyone was there, along with the ex-sicario. Since then, his congregation and other churches in Ciudad Juárez have adopted hundreds of sicarios which has contributed to a marked decrease in the city's notorious murder rate.

The visions and direction Poncho received in the park are the foundation for his growth into a mighty leader of transformation. His gentle smile, under a charming mustache, belies the strength of his fearless ministry in Juárez, formerly the "murder capital of the world." His reach has extended far beyond Juárez through an organization he leads with Daniel Valles called *Avanza Sin Tranza* (Thrive Without Bribes), focused on eliminating corruption in Mexico. Poncho is working on an agricultural guest worker program that will address both the need among Mexicans and those from Central America for jobs, and the US agricultural community's need for workers. He is also helping to organize a new political party in Mexico based on godly principles of government.

The most humorous person in the movement is probably King Flores, of the Philippines. A taxi driver who later went to seminary and is now a businessman, King is what his name suggests: a royal priest!

He and his wife Olive disciple presidents of the Philippines, generals, police chiefs, and mayors. He has led movements to transform cities, states, and the nation.

One such city is Parañaque. When King began, this city was one of the worst in the nation, with garbage stacked high, corruption in all parts of government, and declining tax collection. King led a group that went to city hall to pray for the welfare of the city, and he talked the mayor into letting them pray there daily. They did this for years. Later, the mayor established a church inside city hall because the prayers were being answered!

The city solved its garbage problem, cleaned up its streets, and fixed its crumbling buildings. Crime went down significantly and corruption has been almost eliminated. The city hall signs say, "No Corruption Here." Business has returned to the city and tax collection has multiplied exponentially.

The city was dedicated to God in 2011and this dedication is recorded on its official seal which states, "City of Parañaque, Dedicated to God."

King Flores also discipled Wyden King who has forty motels with a total of 1,400 rooms. The rooms were used by *illicit couples* and were turned over four times a day! This represented a lot of money, but when Jesus came into the picture via King's discipleship, the chain was transformed from "an altar of unrighteousness"— Wyden's own description—to a business dedicated to God.

Now the rooms are only rented to families (couples must show a wedding band or marriage certificate), rooms are prayed over by housekeepers as they're cleaned, the staff prays together, and guests are invited to pray with the staff. The business is prospering and has been reclaimed for the kingdom of God!

Geoff Poon is a millennial entrepreneur in Hong Kong. He was a practicing architect but was led by the Lord to a field he knew nothing about—fashion. As a man of vision, he understood the power of God's Word and envisioned a line of clothes and daily items that had the imprint of scripture on them. The name of his company is AMENPAPA!

Two quotes from their website show their mission:

1. AMENPAPA is a spiritual fashion brand that is driven by a playful childlike hunger to create something that matters to the spirit and have amazing fun while doing it!
2. The very instrument the authorities designed to keep their people oppressed would become the very instrument that God would use to set those people free.

Wanting to create a top fashion brand, Geoff established stores in the highest-end shopping centers of Hong Kong and Singapore. He retains top models, employs great graphics and creates trendy spaces. He gives inspired and creative shows. He even produces plays and supports performing arts events.

Geoff touches the full gamut of the marketplace to spread the Word of God! This is marketplace ministry on steroids!

Catch the Wave

"But God chose the foolish things of the world to shame the wise; God chose the weak things of the world to shame the strong" (1 Corinthians 1:27).

When you grow up in Hawaii, you definitely don't think of yourself as a *world-beater*, like you might in Hong Kong. You think of yourself as inadequate, unqualified, and a nobody. A local phrase *"Who you tink you?"* (Who do you think you are?) is constantly echoing in the back of your mind. If you identify with this, no matter where you're from, these Hawaii stories are for you!

Descendants of a plantation society, Hawaii locals are very humble. This humility has kept our people down, dismissing our own significance in the community and the kingdom of God. Transform Our World Hawaii (TOWH) has helped to transform this perception! These individuals, and many others, are part of the growing army that is committed to fulfilling God's vision for the transformation of Hawaii and beyond!

After the 2004 Harvest Evangelism conference in Argentina, Ed asked three couples to begin a movement of transformation in Hawaii. The couples were Pastor Cal and Joy Chinen, attorney David and Rohnda Monroy, and Caroline and me. Of course, we didn't feel qualified, and the couples didn't know each other well, but we agreed to take it on.

We envisioned a simple plan. Each of us would invite Christian friends to quickly convene a meeting of one hundred people. We would then ask the one hundred to bring ten friends each to a gathering at our convention center. The one thousand would be asked to bring friends to our civic arena. In this way, we thought we'd gather thousands and that we'd do it in just a few months!

Prior to the first gathering of one hundred at New Life Church, we prayed over the facility. As we were scattered over the sanctuary praying, Cal let out a loud grunt, *Ugh!*

We stopped and looked his way. All of us had been intensely praying and the disruption was jarring.

But Cal didn't say anything, so we resumed our prayers. Then Cal let out an even louder *ugh!* He said, "Francis, there's a huge angel here! You're the pastor here. Come and find out what he wants!"

My mind went blank! I walked to the center aisle where Cal was, and into the area he was pointing to. The moment I stepped into the area, a vision came to me! I saw a huge tsunami sweep through a city of dull grey people, buildings, and faded vegetation. After the wave passed, the scene was transformed into a bright colorful community with vibrant people, beautiful buildings, and verdant vegetation! Then, instantly, I was high above looking down on a glowing emerald green island set in a black sea. I saw shadowy forms that looked like canoes departing from the island in all directions. These went to other islands and to continents. Where they touched land, a bright light emerged.

We immediately interpreted this vision to mean the transformation and renewal of Hawaii, but not just Hawaii. We saw that it would go to other lands. It was not to be about us but nations!

We adopted this vision as our calling, and the wave as our logo. It's on the cover of the book, *Catch the Wave of Transformation*, that Caroline subsequently wrote, describing what happened in Hawaii's early transformation movement.

Our first meeting at New Life Church was a success. People were enthusiastic and seemed committed. The second meeting at the Convention Center had eight hundred fifty to nine hundred attendees!

We had booked our arena as an act of faith and held a gathering there that was attended by nearly 2,500 people, including sixty Harvest Evangelism people from around the world. All this in about three months!

The gathering was powerful, with Hawaiian protocol and repentance for the taking of the land from the Hawaiians by the US through annexation. Amazing examples of transformation from international and local participants were shared, and then we commissioned everyone as marketplace ministers. Hawaii has not been the same since.

The vision delivered by the angel began to come to pass immediately after the conference. People left for the four corners of the earth and applied what they learned in Hawaii.

Hawaii began to transform. The vision and call of Daniel Chinen, now a pastor but then a high school student, led to the adoption of most of Hawaii's public schools and regular prayer around the flagpoles of every school campus. Prayer walking also prompted the adoption of streets and communities.

Pastor Cal Chinen, CEO of what is now called Transform Our World Hawaii (TOWH) and senior pastor of Moanalua Gardens Missionary Church for many years, has led the movement in Hawaii. This extraordinary leader has always served as an apostle to other pastors in Hawaii and is now an apostle to TOWH. Joy is his super-sweet wife and Daniel is his son.

While we sometimes jokingly call Cal the "pope" for his passion to disciple Hawaii, he would never say this of himself! He uses the term "plantation spirit" to express the "who you *tink* you" attitude so imbedded in locals, including him. Yet through the power of the Holy Spirit, he heads a group of awesome leaders who are transforming Hawaii!

TOWH is comprised of a core group of a couple dozen pastors and business leaders who meet weekly. We started weekly meetings after King Flores and Brian Burton came to Hawaii and asked us why we weren't getting the results in Hawaii that they were experiencing in the Philippines and Thailand. They asked us how often we prayed together. We responded that we met monthly, or sometimes quarterly. Surprised, they said we had to meet weekly to get results! "You can't get results without commitment. You can't get commitment without giving the meeting priority."

"Impossible!" we responded. "We're too busy!"

We have since found that meeting is a key to having a dynamic movement. You can't have a movement without momentum. You can't have momentum when meeting monthly or quarterly. *Weekly is the minimum in order to develop commitment and momentum!*

In addition to the core TOWH group meeting, there are numerous small group meetings throughout the community. TOWH also had two or three Hawaii conferences a year, each one attended by at least a thousand people. This is in addition to the TOW global conference, now held in Northern California. We are also poised to have quarterly combined church services where all the transformation churches, and those committed to transformation, will gather. *We have finally gained momentum!*

The core of TOWH is ordinary people doing extraordinary things. All would admit that they initially felt God must have made a mistake in choosing them because they were totally unqualified and inadequate, however God has raised them up to disciple the community and beyond to nations! God chooses the right people and we've learned not to second-guess him!

The core group includes Pastor Michele Okimura, a true visionary who has created an international movement called EXPLICIT that deals with sexual issues faced by youth and teens. Although she is shy, Michele's conferences and workshops deal with gender confusion, sex trafficking, sexual abuse, masturbation, and other topics that most pastors wouldn't touch with a ten-foot pole!

EXPLICIT conferences focus on youth but are also attended by parents, youth leaders, and pastors. They have been conducted in Hawaii, the Philippines, Canada, Singapore, and the mainland US to packed audiences! *They are now going viral!*

Pastor Roy Yamamoto is a felon who miraculously was given a third chance. He came to the Lord in prison where he learned to read by reading the Bible! After leaving prison, Roy was led to develop a ministry for the children of the incarcerated. Its signature event is an annual camp where the youth can swim and surf, enjoy great Christian fellowship, and the move of the Holy Spirit. It's called Camp Agape.

Today, thousands of kids attend the camp and receive continued ministry afterwards. Almost 100 percent of the participants leave knowing Jesus and restored to relationship with their fathers! The camps are held on three Hawaiian Islands, in Oregon, Arkansas, and other states. Roy, a quiet and humble man, is now being recognized nationally and internationally.

Roy says that the most powerful part of the ministry is when they take some of the young people into prisons such as Saguaro

Correctional Center in Arizona. When gang leaders see their own kids testifying to the goodness of God, and praising him, even the most hardened go through a radical transformation! The fruit of the ministry has led the Saguaro warden to give them free access to the entire prison, even to those in solitary!

Pastor Jimmy Yamada is a pastor who owns the second largest electrical contracting company in Hawaii (now run by his son). He is an extraordinary thinker and man of vision who has written half a dozen books. Not bad for an electrician who went to public school and not to college!

Jimmy is the "anonymous donor" to many Christian causes, including Camp Agape, as well as the purchase of an entire frontage on the main street of a central Oahu town called Wahiawa for Surfing the Nations (STN), which has the enviable mission of ministering to every *surfable* nation in the world. The transformed block replaced drug houses and porn shops in a district that was known for crime.

Wahiawa is where the largest military installation in Hawaii is, and is a town plagued by the typical issues surrounding military camps with thousands of young men and women. Jimmy's support for the ministry of STN has transformed Wahiawa and touched thousands of young people around the world!

Jimmy and his wife, Diane, pastor a church dedicated to ministering to and housing the homeless. They bought a large property a block from one of the most notorious housing projects in Honolulu and have created a safe place where the homeless are housed and trained in the ways of the Lord to return to society as contributing members.

Diane personally works on teams that cook meals every day for the dozens of people to whom they minister. She and Jimmy tend to people's needs and train them up. With their wealth, Jimmy and Diane could easily afford servants themselves, yet they are servants to those that are considered "the least of these."

These are ordinary people doing truly extraordinary things. (This is the mantra of TOW.)

Four Seasons Resort Lanai, The Lodge at Koele

Four Seasons Resort Lanai at Manele Bay

CHAPTER 5

GOD'S PURPOSE

*And you know that in all things God works for the good of those
who love him, who have been called according to his purpose.*
—Romans 8:28 (NIV)

Miracles in the Marketplace

I became convinced that the miracles we experienced with the
Marriott project were to be our new normal in God's marketplace,
and our firm, Group 70 International (now G70), was to be a marketplace ministry. God was building our faith in the setting of the
marketplace. We came to a point with the Marriott project, however,
when we were owed over one million dollars in fees! This was a lot of
money in those days. It still is!

We couldn't continue to pay our people without funds, so we
prayed. The following day we got a call from Thunder Bay, Canada.
A Canadian company had bought an old hotel on Maui and wanted
us to do a design and construction documents for a 220-unit condo
there. The problem was that there was to be a water moratorium
imposed for the district in six weeks.

They wanted to know if we could do sufficient drawings in
this time to preserve their right to build. After I asked our team
(that had stopped work the day before) whether we could meet the

deadline, it was a *go*, but I stipulated that 10 percent of the fee had to be in our account by the following day. The deposit was made!

We worked frantically for the six weeks and made the submission on time. The final payment of hundreds of thousands of dollars was deposited in our account a few days after the submission. God had given us the cash flow to continue the Marriott drawings!

Amazingly, nothing ever came of the Maui project! There was no follow-up on the permit or on construction. We received a check for over $1 million from the Marriott client soon thereafter! We've always marveled at how this came about and wondered whether there are angels that live in Thunder Bay! *It was certainly a miracle; the new normal!*

We have had other miracles in the office, including healing from cancer, divine provision, and salvation. One of our graphic designers, Joy, had a cold, so I asked if she wanted prayer which she did. I asked if she wanted to give her life to the Lord and she did. We prayed, and she was healed.

Weeks later, however, she found out that she had cervical cancer. We prayed again, and she was healed of the cancer! The doctors told Joy that because of the damage done to her uterus she would not be able to have a child. Well, we prayed again. Today, Joy's daughter Cassidy is an active preteen who loves to dance and participates in sports!

David, a state senator, came to the office to talk about a hydro-electric project with his lawyer, Mark. Just in passing, David asked why it was that when his children prayed for healing, people were healed, whereas when he prayed, they were not. I said that I needed to give him a short lesson on healing, but because Mark was there, I didn't want to take his time. Mark, a nonbeliever, said it was okay, so I launched into a short teaching. I then prayed for David, and while I was praying, the Lord said he'd give David the gift of healing.

I asked David whether he wanted the gift.

"Of course!" he said, so I asked him to stand in an open area in the conference room.

I told Mark to stand behind David, and as I said a simple prayer, David immediately went down, slain in the Spirit!

Mark was shocked but alert enough to catch David and lay him down. I motioned to Mark to join me at the conference table.

After a few minutes, David leaped to his feet and yelled, "I thought it was fake!" I asked him what he meant, and he said that he had seen people go down on TV but thought that they had faked it or were pushed.

Now David had experienced it! "This is what I've been missing!" and from then on he began peppering me with daily e-mails with great enthusiasm.

Mark's father, Stan, was my attorney for many years. He's a senior partner at one of Hawaii's top legal firms and was a regent of the University of Hawaii. Stan told me I'd be surprised by how many times this story has been told in boardrooms in Hawaii!

Much later, I met David and his pastor, Daniel Kikawa, at a Starbucks on the Big Island. We had just gone to a piece of property that David owns to check it out for a religious retreat. Daniel, a good friend, is an author and authority on the history of Christ in Hawaii.

Somehow we got on to the subject of the baptism of the Holy Spirit. It turned out that David had not received the baptism. I was taken aback! How could such a man of God not have the full power of the Holy Spirit?

I asked him if he wanted to receive the baptism.

He asked, "Now? Here?"

"Why not here?" I responded.

I laid hands on him to receive and signs followed!

Why not in the marketplace as much as in the church? Why not in a Starbucks rather than a sanctuary?

Anytime Visions

Relatively few major visions come in my morning time of prayer and envisioning. As I said, this is like a workout. It is preparation to receive God's vision at any time throughout the day.

This was the case for Hanauma Bay Nature Preserve Education Center.

Hanauma Bay is a natural wonder created by God that is formed by the caldera of Koko Head crater, one wall of which has been eroded by the sea to form a beautiful bay, while an abundant reef teeming with life guards the tranquil beach against the rolling surf beyond.

The beauty of Hanauma had led to its degradation. Thousands of tourists were visiting the site every day, killing the coral by walking on the reef, feeding the fish junk food, and polluting the marine environment with sunscreen. Something had to be done.

The mayor of Honolulu called me to talk about this problem. He asked that we do a *world-class* nature preserve center at the rim of the caldera that would educate people about how to behave below. The center would have exhibits that might satisfy some visitors without their going down to the beach.

The very next day, the mayor's managing director, himself an architect, called me and apologetically explained that the mayor wanted a rendering of the facility immediately to include in a slide show of city projects! He knew very well that designing such a facility would normally take weeks, even months, but we had only days.

I was so busy at the time that I asked Steve Yuen, one of our principals, to do the design. Steve is a gifted architect, having gone to Harvard for both his undergraduate and graduate degrees.

Two days later, as I got out of the fifth floor elevator of our office, Steve was waiting for me. He showed me his drawing of a beautiful bird's-eye perspective overlooking the bay. On the rim of the caldera were picturesque Hawaiian grass huts (hale).

I loved the image, but the Holy Spirit told me that no native Hawaiian would build a hale on the rim of Hanauma. No *buildings* belonged there! So I closed my eyes and prayed. Right there in front of the elevator, God gave me a vision. I saw a plaza in front of me at the edge of the caldera that invited me to view the bay and beach below. I looked to the right and saw the land as if lifted, presenting a cave-like entry leading to the education center. I looked to the left and saw the food concession integrated into the hillside.

I did a quick sketch for Steve and asked him to modify his wonderful drawing to reflect this design. The entire interaction took just a few minutes.

A day later, the drawing had been modified, and I went to the city with this design.

The mayor's response was, "Where's the building?"

I said that this was exactly the point!

The buildings were invisible in berms covered with natural grass. In fact, not wanting to excavate any of the land, we built the education center and food concession on the existing ground level and clothed them with artificial rock fabricated in Australia from *skins* made of the exact imprint of the strata of the caldera. From above, you can't see buildings at all! From the sides, the complex looked like an extension of the caldera walls.

The mayor conceded that he had asked for a world-class facility, so he approved God's design. The building never made it into the mayor's slideshow.

When construction began, a protest erupted in the community that was widely reported in the press. People objected vehemently to the construction of buildings on the edge of their beloved Hanauma Bay. The issue made the front pages for days at a time! The outrage lasted until the complex was completed.

When people saw the final product, they embraced and celebrated it! God's design, received in a few minutes in front of the elevator, has since won local and regional design awards.

Hanauma Bay Marine Education Center

Hanauma Bay Marine Education Center Entry

Composite of Hanauma

RENDERING

HANAUMA BAY NATURE PRESERVE
O'AHU, HAWAI'I

You can receive God's vision and plan at any moment, in any place! This was true on the broad slopes of Hualālai volcano on the Big Island of Hawaii. Brokerage magnate Charles Schwab, a world-famous financier George Roberts, and I viewed the site of their future golf course on land formed by a series of lava flows, part vegetated, but part still showing patches of raw lava.

Below were two beautiful and exclusive shoreline resort communities, Hualalai and Kukio, where the rich and famous had their second, third, or fourth homes. The owners of these houses were to be the members of this *invitation-only club*.

The course would be designed by internationally famous golf course architect, David Kitt, who had just done a course at Bandon Dunes, considered by many to be the best new course in America. Kitt subsequently did another eighteen holes at St. Andrews in Scotland.

Chuck and George explained that they had invited me to design the clubhouse for their exclusive golf club because the resort communities below mandated an architectural style that I had popularized called *kama'aina* architecture. This expression incorporates influences of the various cultures that form modern Hawaii. They said, "You're the 'father of kama'aina architecture.'"

Chuck and George explained that grand iconic clubhouses were always mansions, like at St. Andrews. They wanted a beautiful kama'aina-style mansion for their clubhouse. Yet as I viewed the majestic sloping terrain that had not been disturbed by construction, I received a vision from the Lord. It was for something not at all like a traditional mansion. I saw the building emerge like the cinder cones, or "pu'u," that dotted the existing slope. The clubhouse was part of the powerful volcanic landscape, rather than something perched on it and dominating it.

I asked Chuck and George whether they would accept something other than a mansion. They were a bit surprised but open, and just said, "Show us what you mean."

My first task with David was to place the clubhouse in this vast landscape. The Lord led me to a spot at the top of the most recent lava flow marked by a living Kamani tree, the remnant of a forest that once graced the hillside. David agreed to this site and to design the course accordingly. I envisioned the club's social areas at this tip of the lava flow with 240-degree views of four volcanic peaks and the open ocean. The roofs of the social areas were to be *pu'u*-like forms. The interior walls were to be lava as extensions of the flow, with glass panels for the exterior walls that could be easily folded to expose a vast uninterrupted view.

These pu'u would be domes angled to match the angle of the adjacent pu'u. This was a function of the "angle of repose" of the *a'a*, or cinder, that made up the cone. For this reason, the pu'u forms would be unique and only related to this island, on this volcano, and in this flow! These domes would be sheathed with patinaed-copper and glow like the lava of the adjacent pu'u, a bright copper-like orange-gold in the setting sun. The domes would be supported by ohia logs arranged in a forest pattern. Not quite an iconic traditional mansion!

The utilitarian parts of the clubhouse, such as the back of the house, showers, and parking were to be under the lava flow! The flow morphs into lava boulder walls, culminating in the gathering spaces that were covered by the copper domes.

Chuck and George accepted God's design. It was not conventional, in the least, but it has won local and international awards. The Lord's designs are so cool!

Maluhia Composite

KONA PU'U

NANEA GOLF CLUBHOUSE
KAILUA, HAWAII

Nanea Clubhouse Hualalai, Hawaii

Nanea Clubhouse Hualalai, Hawaii

CHAPTER 6

God's Provision

And my God shall supply all your need according
to His riches in glory by Christ Jesus.
—Philippians 4:19

Monsieur President

With God's *vision, faith, opportunity, right people,* and *purpose* will come *provision.* This is more than a tenet of faith, but a practical reality that has been proven to me over and over, like in Tahiti, for example.

My connection with Tahiti began over twenty years ago.

Teiva Raffin, a Tahitian, came to my office to ask if we could collaborate on projects. He was a young architect and I was impressed with his coming all the way to Hawaii to make this connection. I agreed that we could work together.

A few years later, Teiva and I entered a competition for a waterfront park along the harbor edge of Papeete, in Tahiti. The waterfront had been cut off from downtown by a neglected semi-industrial shoreline. We won the competition and I went to Tahiti to look at the site and meet with Teiva regarding the project. Teiva told me that we needed to have an official introductory meeting with the president that would only take about fifteen minutes. It was just a bit of protocol.

At our meeting in the president's office the following day, the Lord showed up! The president asked me what to do with a site on the edge of the harbor called Place Jacques Chirac, a site something like that of the Sydney Opera House, but smaller. For whatever reason, the president had just rejected a competition winner for the site.

The Holy Spirit prompted me to ask what president Chirac's legacy was, and I was told that the French president loved the cultural artifacts of the South Pacific. It seemed natural, therefore, to recommend putting a museum for these cultural artifacts within the very culture that had created them.

The president quickly dismissed the idea, saying that he had another site for such a museum. I responded that while the other site might be fine, a building built there would just be functional, whereas a museum built on this harbor site would become world famous! He immediately changed the subject! A shift occurred in the room and I didn't have a clue why. I was just a visitor and later was told that you don't disagree with the president in public, and in his office!

Yet about ten minutes later, he turned to me and said, "Monsieur Oda, can I ask you a question about the museum? If I put it where you suggest, can it be my idea?" He then smiled and winked at me!

Everyone laughed!

I exclaimed, "Of course, it *IS* your idea!"

Everyone in the room agreed, and at that point we all became friends!

This first fifteen-minute meeting lasted for over an hour, and the president invited me to meet him in his office again at 5:00. This second meeting lasted for one and a half hours!

At the later meeting, the president again asked me about the museum. Getting excited about the prospect, he asked me to show him and the VIPs of Tahiti what I had in mind at a state dinner that would be held in three days! The formal embossed invitations went out the following day!

This was a real problem since the development of drawings for a project like this would normally take weeks! On top of that, we were there for the park project, not for a museum! But what could I do? I prayed.

The next morning, as was our routine, my team of two believers from our office and I jogged and went for a swim before going to Teiva's office. During the swim, God gave me the vision for the museum. It sounds a bit corny, but I swam to the shore, drew the plan in the sand, and then we photographed it!

The museum was to be set on a platform of water, representing the ocean, with the islands of the Polynesian Triangle rising from the sea. The island would hold the galleries of the museum which would be set along the edge of the site so that the water of the platform would visually merge with the harbor.

PORT

ENTRY

PLACE´ JACQUES CHIRAC VUE AERIENNE
PLACE´ JACQUES CHIRAC

It didn't look like any building any of us had ever seen, but it represented Polynesia in a unique way. God's an amazing designer! God's design was based on voyaging, the core of Polynesian culture.

I sent Teiva for research material on Polynesian voyaging—Taputapuatea (focal point for voyaging throughout Polynesia), Rapa Nui (Easter Island), and Aotearoa (New Zealand)—the basic components of the design. God showed us many things we didn't know, but as we did more research, it all came together amazingly well! We worked day and night for the next two days.

Just two hours before we were expected at the president's residence, as we were still putting our slideshow together, we received a call from the president's minister of special projects. He was a French engineer named Jacques. He said that the president also wanted me to propose a solution to Boulevard Pomare. This six-lane boulevard separates downtown Papeete from the shoreline. Seven French engineers had just been in Tahiti studying this problem for six months, and the president had rejected their solution because of the cost. They had proposed tunneling the boulevard fifteen meters below the water table all along the shoreline frontage!

I was shocked at the president's request! I thought, *I'm not a traffic engineer!*

So of course, I prayed. Immediately, a vision came to me that would require the roadway to be lowered only one meter below its existing level and not into the water table. I quickly drew the solution, photographed it, and put it into our slideshow.

The president and his guests were gathered in the private theater on his estate when we arrived. After introductions, we set up our presentation and launched into the slides for the museum. The response was amazement and delight!

The audience was enthralled with this unique solution. Yet as the president complimented me, *I said this was not my design but God's!* Taken aback, he said it was very good nonetheless. I had hoped that the president had forgotten the boulevard, but he asked about it. I projected the slide of my sketch on the screen and the president asked his minister to look at the solution.

"Does it work?" he asked.

Jacque walked up to the screen, inspected the image, and said, "Yes, I think it does."

The president then launched into a humorous criticism of French engineers (Tahitians have a love/hate relationship with the French). He asked, "How could Monsieur Oda come from Hawaii and solve this problem in this short time when French engineers couldn't do it in six months?"

I corrected him politely, "It wasn't me! It was God!"

Throughout the week, this became the leitmotif of our experience: God's miracles! God kept showing up through miraculous and creative solutions to knotty problems!

Three months later, the president called me from Tahiti and asked to know "your God." I introduced him to the Lord on my next visit to Tahiti and baptized him, as well as Teiva and his wife, and Teiva's partner and his wife. They also received the baptism of the Holy Spirit! God reached these people who probably had never entered a church through miracles in the marketplace!

Mahana Beach

The politics of French Polynesia (the name of the country which is divided into five groups of islands with Tahiti being the largest) is complex and convoluted. The president lost his next election and was in and out of office for several years.

Upon his final reelection, based on helping the poor, he announced an international competition to establish a new economic base for tourism in the nation.

While French Polynesia is one of the most beautiful places in the world, its tourism industry was moribund. At one end were luxury resorts on Bora Bora that cost $1,000+ per night for overwater bungalows. On the other end were hotels that were local and not well suited to international tourists. Several midrange hotels had gone out of business because of the lack of critical mass in the middle market.

This competition was to create that critical mass. The hotels were to be on government land on the island of Tahiti that was about two-

FRANCIS S. ODA

thirds the size of Waikiki in Hawaii. The project, called Mahana Beach, was to be built in phases over a seven-year period, essentially all at once!

G70 responded to an international invitation from the French Polynesian government to enter a design competition for the project. We were among eighty-seven companies that entered. Three were selected by the government for the final phase to present their best ideas and designs.

One finalist was a mega-French conglomerate developed around a quasi-governmental bank with design, development, finance, and construction arms. The other was a similar multifaceted mega-Chinese company that even included a famous five-star resort hotel chain. Then there was G70. It was David against two Goliaths!

Through envisioning, God provided us the design and master plan for seven hotels, a convention center, a shopping mall, condos, shops, restaurants, and a park along a promenade paralleling a restructured beach. We presented this in video and 3-D computer drawings.

Composite of Mahana Beach

COCONUT PALM LEAF BASKET

IMPLEMENT OF HOSPITALITY &
GATHERING

MAHANA BEACH COMPETITION
CONVENTION CENTER
TAHITI

HOTEL USING TRADITIONAL BUILDING FORMS

MAHANA BEACH COMPETITION
5-STAR HOTEL
TAHITI

POLYNESIAN VOYAGING CANOE

MAHANA BEACH COMPETITION
6-STAR HOTEL
TAHITI

Through a rigorous process of design juries made up of experts in tourism, economists, engineers, and architects from Paris, we were selected as winners of the competition! Again, with God, David prevailed!

However, at the cocktail party held in Tahiti to announce our selection, the president came to me and asked, "Would you raise the money for the project? We can't do it." I was floored!

Our design was estimated to cost US $3 billion! We were designers in a design competition, not investors or developers! I knew God had put us in this position, so he must have an answer. Whether $3 million, $30 million, $300 million, or $3 billion, what's it matter to God?

We knew that God would raise the funds, and he did, largely through Teiva. Over a period of several years, investors from Hungary, Switzerland, France, the United States, New Zealand, and French Polynesia were gathered for the project!

When God gives you a vision, he will supply the means to accomplish it!

CHAPTER 7

GOD'S FRUIT

By this my Father is glorified, that you bear
much fruit; so you will be My disciples.
—John 15:8 (NKJV)

It turned out that the funds were not the biggest challenge. Because the land belongs to the government, it has taken several years since the competition to get Mahana Beach started. It always takes longer than you think.

The Lord, therefore, had us begin with a hotel on the island of Raiatea on a privately owned parcel. The beautiful beachfront site is adjacent to the *mataina*, or traditional land parcel, that holds the marae Taputapuataea, the historic center of voyaging for all Polynesia. The marae was designated a UNESCO heritage site in early 2018, and because every heritage site must have a good hotel related to it, this hotel was approved for this purpose. The cornerstone was laid in 2019.

THE WESTIN TAPUTAPUATEA
TAHITI

ICONIC MIXED-USE TOWER WITH HOTEL, OFFICE, CONFERENCE & EXHIBITION CENTER

VEHICULAR & PEDESTRIAN GARDEN BRIDGE WITH DINING VENUES & OUTDOOR CAFES

SENTUL CITY, CITY OF GOD
INDONESIA

A second hotel in Papeete (the capital of Tahiti) will begin its design in 2019 and construction in 2020. Two hotels in Bora Bora and one in Moorea will follow. All of this is to be done over a period of six to eight years.

We believe the Lord has provided a process to build the base for tourism, not only on the island of Tahiti, but throughout French Polynesia, and to support the sudden impact of Mahana Beach. This systematic development will also allow us to train our people. *This is important because the primary purpose of the hotels and resorts is not the "bricks and mortar" but to bless the people, the culture and the land.* We say it this way:

1. *Eliminate systemic poverty*—by bringing jobs, training, income to a community.
2. *Address systemic corruption*—by working with noncorrupt individuals and entities and training others in the elimination of corruption.
3. *Honor the local culture*—by strengthening the culture rather than bringing a western overlay to it.
4. *Bless the land*—which often has been damaged to restore God's creation through sustainable and green practices.

The ending of systemic poverty through jobs and small business opportunities is a major objective. In a poor economy, however, the infusion of jobs and money can have unintended consequences.

One such consequence is that many front-of-the-house tourism jobs go to women, while men are in *back-of-house* jobs such as maintenance and groundskeeping, or they remain on the subsistence economy as farmers and fishermen. Wives, therefore, often earn more than their husbands which can shift the dynamics of traditional families. It can lead to family violence!

A focus will be to offset the potential negative consequences for employees and their families through training. My wife Caroline, who is an educator, is in charge of curriculum and faculty for this training. She's drawing faculty from our TOW network who are dealing with issues such as family violence in their own locales. These resource people will work with the local French-speaking trainers.

Pastors Ellie and Becca Kapihe (TOWH pastors) will be among the teachers addressing family violence. Ellie and Becca, who have ministered to families and churches in French Polynesia and Rapa Nui, are familiar with violence in Polynesian families (their own) and how God can turn this around!

Their beautiful older daughter went from being a top student to barely scraping by and she began to run away from home. Ellie and Becca's family was transformed as they applied the godly principles they will teach. They have even gone on TV in Hawaii to give their testimony!

Ellie points out that, even as a pastor, he didn't understand that the old Polynesian ways were not right! It was deeply imbedded in the culture that a good parent literally beat their children into submission! The Kapihes now have God's culture of honor at home. Their children are again excelling, and both Becca and Ellie are honoring their children and being honored in return.

Financial training in Tahiti will include household finance, small business development, buying a home, and other issues that will help families to prosper. Going from a partial subsistence to a cash economy must be managed for it to be a blessing and not a curse! A common stronghold in every culture and society is corruption. It's experienced at every level—personal, organizational, and governmental—and French Polynesia is no exception.

Poncho Murguia and Daniel Valles, from TOW Mexico, will be our experts, training the trainers. They have taught thousands of people in Mexico to "thrive without bribes"! Governments, businesses, and universities in Mexico have ongoing training through Poncho and Daniel's program, *Avanza Sin Tranza*.

We intend for the resorts to be "corruption-free zones." We plan to extend training to purveyors of goods and services to the hotels, to shop owners, and to operators. We hope to get the cooperation of the local and national governments. Corruption is a cancer that must be healed for the body of the community to thrive!

Training in cultural practices, arts, crafts, as well as in how to sustain the land and sea, is also part of God's vision for French Polynesia. Caroline will use her curriculum training and love of the French language to bless the people, first in Raiatea and then across the rest of French Polynesia.

There seems to be a reason why the Lord had us scale the projects smaller to larger. Starting with the Mahana Beach project (with seven hotels) over a few years would have been difficult, if not impossible, to manage from this training perspective. While the buildings may be built rather quickly, the people cannot change as fast.

The plan is to train the Raiatea staff first and have them practice their new skills. Then we'll have them train the staff of the next hotel. The staffs of both hotels would then train the staff of the next two hotels. When we get to the big Mahana project, we'll have the human infrastructure in place to truly disciple a community and then a nation.

Do we know how to do this? Not really. Have we done this before? No! So are we qualified? Definitely not! Yet we know that God has given us his vision, and we're chosen to implement it! That's all we need to know!

CHAPTER 8

ENVISIONING BEYOND IMAGINATION

See, I am doing a new thing! Now it springs up; do you not perceive it?
I am making a way in the wilderness and streams in the wasteland.
—Isaiah 43:19

Impostor

I was raised in Palama, one of the poorest neighborhoods in Honolulu. To call it a poor neighborhood is being polite; others would call it a slum. We lived across from the worst housing projects in the city. It was a tough neighborhood.

My father was a struggling artist, but my family was strong. I only spoke Pidgin English until I was twelve years old, not realizing that there was any other way to speak! I knew no Caucasian children.

Entering junior high at the University of Hawaii's lab school, where they trained future teachers, I stepped into a new world. The races were mixed and everyone, even local kids like me, spoke this strange language called Standard English! I was embarrassed and kept my mouth shut for months!

This was when I learned about the "impostor syndrome," even if I didn't call it that at the time. I felt that the school had made a mistake by admitting me (I found out later that, in fact, as a training program for future teachers, they were seeking pidgin speakers to approximate the profile of public schools). In any case, I felt like an impostor.

Around that time, my father bought the bar that was in front of our dilapidated house. This was a big surprise to all of us, especially to my mother. After all, what did my father know about the bar business? He was an artist! His art shop was in our garage.

I have a vivid image of those days—lying in my bed in a room shared with my two brothers and grandmother, staring at an area of the ceiling that was nicely painted and "busted up"! It was about a square foot in size. I wondered whether one day I'd live in a house that was as nice as that square foot of ceiling!

Amazingly, the bar became quite successful, allowing us to move to a much better neighborhood during my high school days. Our home was, in fact, quite nice, and all of it was like the square foot of ceiling! I wonder if this was an early hint of envisioning with God.

That bar also allowed my parents to pay for my going to Cornell University! I wanted to be an architect, not knowing anything about architecture nor knowing any architects. Cornell was and still is rated number one in architecture, but who knew at the time? It was God since I had not applied to any school but intended to go to the University of Hawaii.

The UH had offered me a scholarship and a special program where I would design my own curriculum. They promised I would graduate in three years!

One day, my master teacher at the lab school (the teacher of the student teachers) asked me what colleges I had applied to. When I said, "None. I'm going to UH," she flipped out and almost dragged me into her office! She asked what applications I had in my desk since we had done a writing unit for applications. The only one I had was Cornell! She filled out the application that afternoon and called my parents to sign it that evening. I returned it to school and she sent it in.

It was already two weeks past the deadline, but a few weeks later I received an acceptance!

Up to this time, no one in my family had been to college; we were clueless. Moreover, no one had ever been to the mainland US. We were socially, culturally, and physically isolated.

Cornell was a mega impostor situation! My sixty architecture classmates were all in the top 98 percent of the nation, as was I. However, they knew how to study and had taken advanced courses. Many had gone to elite prep schools in Europe, England, or the US. They were way ahead of me in discipline, knowledge, and maturity. I was a duck out of water!

Architecture school turned out to be one continuous sleepless sprint. We lost people left and right. All were bright, but many didn't have the creativity or endurance to cross the finish line. By the time we graduated, from the original sixty, and twenty more who had "busted down" from earlier years, there were only eleven of us standing! Yet from our class of eleven, one became dean of the school of architecture at Yale, another dean at Princeton, one an eminent professor at Harvard, and all have become prominent practitioners. If one is to be an impostor, this was a great group with which to "fake it until you make it!"

Family

As a young architect practicing in San Francisco and Berkeley, California, I would dream wonderful designs that I would then draw. My professors at Cornell had imbedded the idea that the designs were inside us and what we had to do was get them out. This was the challenge for me, and God later showed me it was a lie.

I did my internship in San Francisco and then formed a practice in Berkeley called Quinn and Oda while Caroline attended graduate school. After receiving her BA at Stanford, she was doing a Master of Social Work at UC Berkley. We loved it there!

My partner, Pat Quinn, was vice chair of the college of environmental design at UC Berkeley, and he later became dean of the school of architecture at Rensselaer Polytechnic Institute (RPI). Born and educated in Ireland, he's a wonderfully gifted teacher, designer, artist, and person.

Pat and I won many design awards and gained renown early on. I was twenty-five years old, and Pat was forty. This early success made Caroline and me wonder, *Is this it? Is this what it was all about?*

Caroline and I searched for answers in paths like encounter, Zen meditation, and EST, yet very soon after we began a new thing, we would see problems and questions in the activities that had promised answers.

We needed answers. Our marriage was stressed (as two first born children, we were both accustomed to getting our way), and our education didn't help either (Stanford and UC Berkeley for her and Cornell for me). We were too smart for our own good, or so we acted!

That is why the encounter with God through Roy and Joan was so critical for us. It not only changed our lives, but it also saved our family. Unlike the other things we had tried, our relationship with the Lord has grown stronger as we've pursued it. Rather than finding problems, we've found solutions; rather than questions, we've found answers!

Caroline had gotten two graduate degrees (now three with a PhD). She was blessed in a very successful professional life that finally led to her being the head of St. Andrews School in Honolulu. This school, established in 1867 by a Hawaiian queen, has a rich history, and it was her high school alma mater.

Caroline understood that she was to do two major things at St. Andrews School, in addition to building on its high academic standing. She was to reignite the flame of the Lord which had waned after the sisters who founded and ran the school for close to 150 years had all passed on. She was also to reimbue the love for the Hawaiian culture that had been largely overlooked for a century.

Certain of her calling, she prayed. Believing staff members and parents came alongside. Talking to these Christians, she learned that they may have prayed Caroline in rather than the other way around!

Caroline took specific steps to make the school more Hawaiian. She studied the Hawaiian language and became almost fluent. She engaged a master teacher of hula, a *Kumu Hula*, to impart the love of the culture to the students. She revived ceremonies that honored the Hawaiian monarchs who had established the school—Queen Emma and King Kamehameha IV.

With this focus, Caroline was asked to sit on one of the most significant boards in Hawaii, the Queen's Medical Center. This is Hawaii's largest and only quaternary hospital and the backbone of medical services in Hawaii. It, too, was founded by King Kamehameha IV and Queen Emma.

As a board member, she prayed for a greater expression of the Christian heritage of the founders of the hospital, as well as a greater expression of the Hawaiian culture. This she did in her prayer closet.

Over time, both these prayers were answered at Queen's Medical Center, as were the prayers for the school. As Caroline persisted in prayer, not only was prayer reinstituted at board meetings and hospital gatherings, but hospital leaders began to share their faith openly. The hospital now has no limitation of expressions of faith and expresses its Hawaiian heritage at gatherings with chants, mele (song), and protocol.

Caroline's call has now extended globally. She was asked by Ed Silvoso to develop an educational arm within our TOW movement called Transformation University, or TU, and Caroline was designated its chancellor. Concurrently, Caroline earned a PhD in curriculum development for distance education since this was the primary mode of instruction for the university.

Today's classes are held with students from Africa, Europe, North America, Asia, and Australia in real time and through online podcasts. The faculty is similarly gathered from throughout the world. Caroline was commissioned as an apostle within the movement in 2017, and she is truly an apostle to the nations both physically and virtually!

Our daughter Nalani (which means "from heaven" in Hawaiian) was an English teacher in Japan for several years after college, then a semi-professional kite-boarder who competed around the world! Coming home from one of her competitions, she had a terrible toothache. It was Saturday and she couldn't go to her normal dentist so called the dentist father of one of her best friends and high school classmates. He opened his office to treat her, and upon her return, Nalani announced that she wanted to be a dentist!

The problem was that her undergraduate degree was in anthropology, so she had to make up courses like organic chemistry at the University of Hawaii to study for her medical boards. She then chose the University of the Pacific program in San Francisco for her training and now has her own practice in Portland, Oregon.

Our son Reid has a musical passion. After having advanced status out of high school, he dropped out of college in the second year to pursue a career in music. We were troubled. It was not so much the music, but the related lifestyle. We prayed.

The Lord showed us that Reid was to be the third generation of artists in our family—my father, myself and Reid, albeit in different media. I flew to the University of Colorado to give him his mother's and my blessing. Reid said that he'd remain in music for ten years, and if he didn't *make it*, he would be back to school!

We began to pray for him on the phone weekly during the ten years and thereafter, using the Shabbat Prayer that Jewish parents pray over their children. We had learned about it through TOWH.

Ten years later, he came to us and said he was going back to school! I was surprised and asked him why since he made a good living and had even scored a movie, stage show, and had produced several records. I had forgotten about his promise, though his mother remembered it!

Starting at the bottom, Reid clawed his way from San Francisco Community College to do a BA at UC San Diego. That was when Princeton offered him a full ride toward a PhD, gave him an annual stipend, an acoustical laboratory and a *laptop* band to play anything he composed! A real God story!

After seven years, Reid graduated from Princeton with a PhD in computer science and now works for Google. Amazingly, his musical interest shaped his research and allowed him to get a patent during his schooling in what he calls the "Universal Metronome," a way for musicians to overcome acoustical delay when playing together over the internet. Who would have thought he could use his love of music to fuel his career!

Reid is married to Erin Hartman, PhD, a professor at UCLA. They met when she was a postdoctoral student at Princeton and are true soulmates! Erin, who is from Austin, is a true Texas girl who can change a car tire and weld, as well as cook and solve advanced algorithmic problems!

Not to be left behind by the family, I also have a doctor of architecture from the University of Hawaii. My dissertation was an extension of the passion the Lord had given me for the incorporation of culture into modern architectural design. The title was "Architects: Keepers of the Culture Designing in the Cultural Landscape."

I sometimes marvel that we grew from being a family that had never gone to college (on the Oda side), shaped by the "who you *tink* you" culture, to a family where everyone has gone beyond what they could have dreamed or imagined. We're products of God's culture!

Indonesia

But it's all for a purpose—God's purpose!

During our commissioning ceremony, Ed Silvoso explained that the term "apostle" was a secular title in Roman culture that referred to a general or admiral who was given a fleet of ships with cargo and craftsmen to go and build a replica of Rome in a colony to represent the presence of the emperor.

Christian Apostles go far and wide to build the kingdom of God and represent the Lord's presence. The Lord has me doing this in Indonesia. When we go to nations to design and build, we do it in the name of the Lord. We do projects and cities dedicated to God. We train people in kingdom principles and establish outposts of the kingdom throughout the world.

It follows, therefore, that not all the people I work with are Christians. Jesus's command to "make disciples of all nations" (Matthew 28:19, NKJ), I believe, directs us to disciple all those in a nation, not just as believers! After all, there were no Christian nations in Jesus's day or, arguably, today.

The Lord made this point when calling me to Indonesia—an 87 percent Muslim nation with the largest Muslim population in the world! I was not to do a typical missions project to speak or help build a church or school, but I was to design and develop cities! Not just one, but two cities—Sentul and Jonggol. Both dedicated to God!

The cities are the vision of a TOW businessman, Cahyadi Kumala, who asked me to help him envision the planning and design of these cities. They are situated in the uplands that form the watershed of Jakarta and are about forty-five minutes to an hour from the capital on a good traffic day. Sentul City has been developing for over a decade and includes commercial, hospitality, and residential enclaves in a green and lush environment. It's a garden city dedicated to sustainability and a healthy lifestyle for its residents.

Jonggol is thirty thousand hectares, or a little less than seventy-five thousand acres. That's a lot of land! It's adjacent to Sentul City and, as yet, undeveloped.

God really surprised us at the beginning of the Jonggol project when we were to plan the central business district (CBD). Hitoshi Hida, one of the principals of G70 (and the Japanese ministry leader at New Life Church), and I arrived in Jakarta to meet with Cahyadi and the prior planners of Jonggol. They were from the Jakarta office of the largest planning firms in the world. They presented their work to us and gave me a huge bound book that illustrated and presented analysis and data for their master plan. It was impressive!

The following morning, we planned to go to the site selected by them for the CBD. As I do every morning, I envisioned with God. That morning, however, I just sat looking at what seemed to be a white concrete wall. It was that way for a while, and I figured that the Lord would show me a vision soon.

After about five or ten minutes, I asked the Lord what was going on.

He said, "I'll speak to you at the site."

When I told Hitoshi this at breakfast, he was very concerned and asked what our client would say. He was accustomed to God giving us a vision, drawing it up and presenting it to the client. This time we would be empty-handed!

The project manager picked us up and we spent about three and a half hours, first on highways, then dirt roads, winding our way to the site of the CBD. We finally stopped at a pleasant gently sloping area filled with the trees of an old rubber plantation. I liked it.

The moment I stepped out of the four-wheel drive vehicle, however, the Lord spoke and said, "This is the wrong site!" Without thinking, I turned to the project manager and said, "This is the wrong site."

With an astonished look on his face, he asked how I knew.

I said, "God just told me!"

The project manager must have thought that I was out of my mind since I knew nothing about the project! I had just gotten off the plane, whereas he and the planners had worked on it for years! He must have thought, *Who is this crazy guy that Mr. Kumala brought from Hawaii?*

I asked him for a map, and as I looked at it, the Lord pointed out the site for the CBD. I pointed to it and said, "This is the site!" The project manager didn't even ask me how I knew.

I determined later that God's site was about 7.2 km (four and a half miles) from where we were standing. Jonggol is very rough country with rivers, valleys, and peaks. The land that separated us from the location I was pointing to could not be reached from where we were, nor could it be reached from any existing road!

Our trip back to Jakarta was quiet. I did not have much of an appetite for dinner upon arrival at our hotel, but I did review the master plan book that I had been given the day before. One very good aspect of the master plan was it had gridded the vast Jonggol lands with a detailed analysis of each square of the grid. Comparing the gridded map to the one I had marked on the site, I located God's CBD location. It turned out to be a very developable site.

The next morning, I met with the prior planners. I complimented them on their report but said that I disagreed with their conclusion about the location of the CBD. I asked them why they had selected it. It turned out that it was the selection of the prior owner of the land for reasons they didn't know. I asked them about the site that God had shown me, and they said that it was also a good site. In fact, it was a site that would be close to a major government road that was under construction. This would allow access soon, whereas the original site would not be accessible with a good road for many years.

The following day, upon his return from Singapore to Jakarta, I told Cahyadi about what happened. His emphatic response was that we'd go with God's site. I described to him what God had shown me the moment I pointed to his location on the map. I had received God's vision like a video.

I saw myself approaching the CBD area through some rice fields. A unique bridge went over a river, connecting to a river-walk road lined with cafes, hotels, shops, and boutiques. This led to the main street going up a slight hill. The main street was flanked with offices, stores, restaurants, and other amenities. At the top of the hill was a museum of art. At the juncture of the river-walk road and the main street was an outdoor performance venue. Cahyadi loved it!

Analyzing the area using drone views and satellite photos, we determined that there were rice paddies in the approach to the CBD, a river, and a hill. Only God knew!

At the office in Jakarta, as I entered the conference room where the prior planners were seated, they exclaimed, *"You picked the best site!"* They had done a thorough analysis of the new site. I said, *"It's not my site but God's!"* They pointed to a small inset on one page of their original master plan report. It was a picture of the CBD site chosen by the planning group that had preceded them. In the vast expanse of Jonggol, it was exactly God's site!

The planning and development of both cities will continue for decades. Funds from Sentul City currently support three schools for Muslim children living in the villages that have *squatted* on the lands. Modern agricultural techniques have been taught to the subsistence farmers, tilling the Sentul and Jonggol lands with spectacular results. A new potable water system has been developed for the squatter villages, and the work goes on. The Lord reminds us all that it's not about bricks and mortar but about people and his kingdom.

Indonesia Innovation City Sentul

Indonesia Innovation City Sentul

You Can Do It Too!

If the scale and scope of some of these projects of God seem a bit daunting to you, join the club! That's how I felt at the beginning of envisioning with God! I assure you that you'll get used to it!

The Lord will always give you visions beyond your imagination! He will give you God-sized visions, not ones tailored to your comfort level. At first, it's quite normal to feel like an impostor, or to feel like God made a *mistake* in choosing you because you're not qualified!

Rest assured, you're not, and God knows it! Get this clearly in your spirit. You're not qualified, but you are *chosen. With being chosen, God provides all the qualities you need!*

As you've seen, it began with *God's vision* and *God's Word* I received on the freeway that fateful morning. With vision, came *faith*; faith proclaimed the vision to the people in the office despite their doubt. *There's power in proclamation!*

Vision and faith brought *opportunity* by the end of the week. Faith in God's vision, I now understand, is essential to even recognize the opportunity, for if you are not looking for something, you'll rarely find it. *Believing is seeing, not the other way around!*

With *vision, faith*, and *opportunity* come the *right people*, such as Johnny.

The right people are not attracted just by the opportunity, but the opportunity provides the ways and mean to employ their talents. *The right people are attracted by the vision, not money.* Be sure you have the right people on the bus. With *vision, faith, opportunity*, and the *right* people, God's *purpose* is clarified.

In the Marriott case, I believe a purpose was the fulfillment of the prophecy and the launching of our practice around the world based on God's vision. *Personally, the greatest purpose was to confirm that I could take the Word of God as truth.*

With vision, faith, opportunity, the right people, and purpose come *resources*. God's purpose attracts resources. Even when resources are delayed in coming, the Lord can direct them through unexpected sources like Thunder Bay, or as with Mahana, from around the world! You don't have to chase your tail to get resources. If God proclaims it in a vision, he will fund it. Pastor Allen Cardines says, *"If it's God's will, it's God's bill!"*

Finally, comes *fruit*—tangible results—like building Marriott's first resort hotel, the most successful in its chain for a decade! "You will eat the fruit of your labor; blessings and prosperity will be yours" (Psalm 128:2, NIV).

This *vision package* is what I've come to expect and to rely on. Its value is that, understanding the pattern, I don't have to stress and strive to get to the next step, like finding the right team or getting financing for a program. I can trust God to provide what is needed, at the right time, in the right way, as long as I'm diligently following his vision!

As I said before, believing is seeing, not the other way around. Believe what God shows and tells you, then follow the path and believe that God will use you in mighty ways. If he can do it with me, with my very humble beginnings, he certainly can and will do it with you! "He guides the humble in what is right and teaches them his way" (Psalm 25:9, NIV). Envision with God and your life will never be the same!

CPSIA information can be obtained
at www.ICGtesting.com
Printed in the USA
JSHW050144220822
29396JS00004B/62